GIFT FROM CLA
10 50TH ALUMNI

THROUGH DIFFICULTIES
TO THE STARS

PER ARDUA AD ASTRA

Reflections Of God's Faithfulness
Over an 80-Year Journey

AYORINDE IDOWU

PER ARDUA AD ASTRA
*Reflections Of God's Faithfulness
Over an 80-Year Journey*

Copyright ©2025 by Ayorinde Idowu

Paperback ISBN: 978-1-965593-35-6

All rights reserved. No part of this publication may be reproduced, distributed, or transmitted in any form or by any means, including photocopying, recording, or other electronic or mechanical methods without the prior written permission of the author except in the case of brief quotations embodied in reviews and certain other non-commercial uses permitted by copyright law.

Published by Cornerstone Publishing

A Division of Cornerstone Creativity Group LLC
Info@thecornerstonepublishers.com
www.thecornerstonepublishers.com

Author's Contact

To book the author to speak at your next event or to order bulk copies of this book, please, use the information below:

ayorinde_idowu@hotmail.com

Printed in the United States of America.

DEDICATION

I dedicate this book as a legacy to my children, grandchildren, and future generations—so that they may see and believe in the power of God. My journey is confirmation of the fact that life is not without challenges, but every difficulty holds the seed of a triumph.

No matter the trials we face, God remains ever-present, shaping our lives in ways we may not always understand in the moment. The main objective is to evangelize to the world, and based on my experiential knowledge on the faithfulness of God, encourage brethren to never give up on their aspirations in life, but persevere and trust in God always.

CONTENTS

DEDICATION v
ACKNOWLEDGMENTS ix
PREFACE xii

1. Floodgates Of Joy 1
2. Treasured Heritage 9
3. Educational Foundations 21
4. The "Per Ardua" Factor 35
5. My American Visa Miracle 45
6. Realities Of An Immigrant 55
7. A Mighty Escape 67
8. Greater Heights 79
9. Heeding Nigeria's Call To Service 91
10. Further Exploits At NNPC 103
11. Divine Awakening 113

12. Deeper Fellowship And Spiritual Service 125

13. From Science To Scripture: Journey Into Kingdom Writing 133

CLOSING THOUGHTS 142

ACKNOWLEDGMENTS

With a heart full of gratitude, I give thanks to the Almighty God, whose unfailing grace and mercy have made this autobiography possible. He alone deserves all the glory, honor, power, and majesty. Looking back at the journey that has brought me to this milestone, I am overwhelmed by His faithfulness. It is by His divine enablement that I have been able to complete this work, and I am especially grateful that I can present it as a testimony of His goodness on the occasion of my 80th birthday.

My deepest appreciation goes to my beloved wife, Olawunmi, whose incredible support, patience, and encouragement have been instrumental in my life's journey. She has been my confidant, my partner in faith, and my constant source of strength. To our wonderful children, their spouses, and our precious grandchildren, I extend my heartfelt gratitude. Your encouragement, prayers, and persistent reminders played a significant role in bringing this autobiography to life.

I particularly appreciate my dear son, Pastor Babatunde, whose words of encouragement ignited the desire in me to document this journey. After I successfully wrote and published four scriptural books in 2018, he urged me to take the next step by writing this autobiography. Though it took another six years before I finally embarked on this project, his words never left me. My children's eagerness to know more about my upbringing, the places I lived, and the many ways God shaped my life was a major motivation to complete this work.

Throughout my journey, God has placed extraordinary people in my life—mentors, friends, colleagues, spiritual leaders, and members of my faith community—who have been His vessels in guiding, uplifting, and supporting me through various seasons of life. Many of their names appear throughout these pages, and to each one of them, I say: thank you. Your kindness, prayers, and encouragement have left an indelible mark on my life, and I pray that God, in His infinite grace, will bless you abundantly for being part of my story.

This autobiography is not merely the story of my life, but a testimony of God's faithfulness. To everyone who has played a role—whether great or small—I appreciate you deeply. May God reward you richly and continue to use you for His glory.

PREFACE

For years, my immediate family—especially my children and grandchildren—have expressed a deep curiosity about my life's journey. They wanted to know not just the broad strokes of my history but the intricate details of how and where I grew up, the challenges I faced, and the ways in which the Lord led me through different seasons of life.

Their eagerness stemmed from a desire to understand the realities of education, family life, career development, and the general experience of growing up in Nigeria during my time. They often wondered how the socioeconomic environment shaped my generation and how we navigated life's hurdles with the limited resources available to us.

This autobiography is my attempt to document these reflections—not just as a historical record, but as a testimony of God's faithfulness in my life. Across the span of eight decades, I have experienced divine protection, provision, and guidance. There were moments when the path ahead seemed uncertain, particularly after I completed my secondary school education. With no apparent financial sponsorship to pursue higher learning, the future looked bleak. Yet, God, in His infinite mercy, sent helpers at every critical junction. Time and again, He made a way where there seemed to be none, proving that His faithfulness never wavers.

I write this book as a legacy for my children, grandchildren, and future generations—so that they may see and believe in the power of God. My journey is a confirmation of the fact that life is not without challenges, but every difficulty holds the seed of a triumph. No matter the trials we face, God remains ever-present, shaping our lives in ways we may not always understand in the moment.

The foundation of this book aligns with the divine instruction in Habakkuk 2:2-3, which says: *"Then the LORD answered me and said: 'Write the vision and make it plain on tablets, that he may run who reads it. For the vision is yet for an appointed time; but at the end it will speak, and it will not lie. Though it tarries, wait for it, because it will surely come, it will not tarry.'"*

These words remind me that no matter how long it takes, God's promises are sure. Though obstacles may arise, though adversity may try to hinder the fulfillment of a vision, God's purpose will always come to pass in His perfect timing.

As you journey through the pages of this book, may you be inspired to trust in God's faithfulness and remain steadfast in the pursuit of your life's purpose. If my experiences serve as an encouragement to even one person—to hold on, to keep the faith, and to walk in obedience to God—then my purpose in writing this book will have been fulfilled.

Ayorinde Idowu

1
FLOODGATES OF JOY

On Sunday, April 29, 1945, joy erupted like a wellspring in the household of Mr. James Ojo Idowu in the ancient town of Ado-Ekiti, the heart of what is now Ekiti State, southwestern Nigeria. The news had just filtered in that my mother, Mrs. Emily Omolola Idowu, had given birth to a healthy baby boy.

In Yoruba culture, the birth of a child is always a joyous occasion, but my birth carried an even deeper significance. For four years, my parents had waited, prayed, and hoped for another child. Though they were devoted Anglicans who trusted in God's will, they could not ignore the unspoken weight of societal expectations.

In a world where children were seen as the crowning glory of a marriage, having only one child was often viewed as a limitation. My elder sister, Kikelomo—whose name meant "Born to be Cherished"—had been their first blessing, but as the years passed without another child, whispers of concern must have begun to stir. Would she remain an only child? Would my parents' hopes for a growing family be unfulfilled?

And then I came.

My arrival was more than a birth—it was a declaration that the doors of blessing had swung open again. True to Yoruba tradition, my parents chose names that reflected the circumstances of my birth. They called me *Ayorinde*—"Joy has Come"—because that was exactly what I represented to them. I was also named *Olusegun*—"The Lord has Conquered"—as a testimony of triumph over years of waiting, and *Oluwemimo*—"The Lord has Purified Me"—a name that carried the weight of spiritual renewal and answered prayers.

But my story didn't begin and end with my parents' joy. According to my mother, the Israeli doctor who delivered me—a man who was not only a physician but also a pastor—looked upon me and spoke some prophetic words that would linger in her heart for years to come. "This child will grow to be a calm and successful man," he said with certainty.

My birth not only relieved my parents of the burden of waiting, but it also reassured them that the floodgates had been reopened for more children. And just as they believed, more blessings followed. In 1947, my younger sister, *Oluyemisi*—"The Lord has Honored Me"—was born. A few years later, my youngest sibling arrived, another girl named *Olayinka*—"I'm Surrounded by Wealth"—whose birth completed our family's circle of love and promise.

BALANCED UPBRINGING

I spent the first five years of my life in Ado-Ekiti, and while I do not have many vivid memories from that time, certain impressions remain engraved in my mind. My family lived in the staff quarters of an Anglican school, where both of my parents were teachers. The quarters were part of a vast Anglican Diocese campus, a well-structured enclave that housed schools, churches, and residential buildings.

It was a self-contained world, offering little exposure

to the life beyond its borders. Yet, within that enclosed environment, my earliest experiences were shaped by faith, discipline, and an atmosphere of warmth and love.

According to my mother, I was a calm but highly curious child—active, communicative, and constantly asking questions. The moment I learned to speak, I bombarded everyone with questions, sometimes without even waiting for answers. But beyond my inquisitiveness, what stands out most in my recollection of those early years is the deep love that filled our home.

This love was evident not only in the way my parents nurtured us but also in the names they gave each of their children. In Yoruba culture, names carry deep meanings, often reflecting the circumstances of a child's birth or the aspirations of the parents. My siblings and I bore names that spoke of joy, honor, and divine blessings, a reflection of how our parents viewed us—not just as children but as precious gifts to be cherished. We were raised with this same sense of value and belonging, knowing that we were deeply loved and celebrated.

SEASONS OF MERRIMENT

Our home came alive with festivities during Christmas and Easter. Those seasons were filled with joy and excitement, as our parents went to great lengths to make them special. They ordered clothing, shoes, biscuits, and animated toys from England by mail, and our celebrations always included the slaughtering of chickens and goats for feasts of rice and pounded yam. My mother, a gifted and trained cook, prepared delicious treats—coconut candies, special biscuits, *chin-chin*, and other delicacies that we eagerly looked forward to. However, these were not merely indulgences; they were often used as incentives to encourage us to excel in our studies and truly earn the enjoyment of the holidays.

But, as I noted earlier, while our childhood was filled with warmth and celebration, it was not without structure, discipline, and the inculcation of strong values. My parents, though loving, were strict disciplinarians. This was to be expected for several reasons. First, as I will be revealing in the next chapter, both came from a lineage of religious leaders and moralists; they were raised in homes where discipline was not just a principle but a way of life.

Second, as firstborns in their respective families, my parents had been brought up with high expectations and had, in turn, learned to lead with firmness from a young age. Third, as devoted Anglicans, they lived by biblical principles and expected the same of their children. Finally, as educators responsible for molding the lives of countless students, they naturally held their own children to the highest standards.

Despite the discipline, our relationship with our parents was built on mutual respect and deep affection. My mother, with her nurturing nature, was naturally easier to bond with. She showered us with tenderness, making our home a haven of warmth. My father, on the other hand, embodied the quintessential African patriarch—loving yet firm, guiding with a steady hand and leaving little room for laxity. He believed in discipline as a means of shaping character and instilling a sense of responsibility in us.

LASTING LEGACIES

Through both their words and their example, my parents instilled in us core values that have remained with me throughout my life. They taught us to be content with what we had, to respect our elders, to love and cooperate with our peers, and to uphold integrity in all things. More than anything, they emphasized perseverance—never giving up, no matter how difficult the journey might seem.

To reinforce these lessons, my parents ensured that we had dedicated family time for prayer, Bible study, and meaningful discussions. Church attendance was non-negotiable; we attended services regularly and punctually. They themselves were deeply involved in the church and the community, leading by example. Both taught in various church groups, and their commitment extended beyond our local parish. My parents served on the Parochial Church Council (PCC), the highest administrative body within the national Anglican dioceses. This council, composed of clergy, churchwardens, and lay representatives, played a crucial role in the governance of the church.

My father was also the church's regular organist, a role he took very seriously. It became our duty to carry his Bible and music sheets ahead of him, ensuring everything was in place for Sunday services. In this way, we were not just passive participants in church life; we were actively engaged in the responsibilities that came with it.

But beyond the discipline, values, and structured upbringing, my parents had a heart for others. Our home was always open to those in need, and we grew up alongside other children whom my parents took in and nurtured as their own. This culture of kindness and generosity left a profound impact on me. It shaped not only my personal values but also influenced the way I raised my own children.

To this day, serving in church leadership has become a way of life. All my children are deeply rooted in faith, holding pastoral and ministry positions. Even my grandchildren are actively involved in children's and youth Christian fellowships.

Looking back, I realize that the foundation my parents laid in those early years continues to bear fruit across generations. The legacy of faith, love, discipline, and service they instilled in us remains unbroken.

2
TREASURED HERITAGE

I cannot fully recount the experiences, values and principles that have shaped and guided me through life without acknowledging the pivotal role played by my grandparents. Their influence ran deep, not just in my upbringing but in the very fabric of my family's legacy.

My paternal grandfather, Baba Agba Idowu, was a native of Ogbomoso, hailing from the Ogunlude Compound in Akata, present-day Oyo State. He was married to my grandmother, Mama Ajesunmo (or Ojesunmo, as she was sometimes called). They shared a strong and happy union, bonded by love, faith, and a commitment to raising a God-fearing family.

As devout Anglicans, they were deeply involved in church activities, instilling religious discipline in their children—a tradition that would be passed down through the generations.

Grandpa Idowu was a man of firm principles, a strict disciplinarian whose life revolved around duty, honor, and justice. He served as a police officer, known for his forthrightness and commitment to maintaining law and order. His exceptional dedication to duty led to his transfer to Ado-Ekiti, where he was tasked with handling land-related issues as a Local Government policeman. This relocation marked a significant turn in our family's history, as it was in Ado-Ekiti that he would establish roots and raise his children, including my father.

During his years in Ado-Ekiti, Grandpa ensured that my father received a solid education, supporting him through high school and nurturing his thirst for knowledge. Driven by an innate passion for learning and a desire to fulfill his life's purpose, my father eventually returned to Oyo to enroll at St. Andrew's College, Oyo—now Emmanuel Alayande University of Education. Established in 1896 by the Church Missionary Society (CMS), it was Nigeria's first and oldest teachers' training college, producing generations of educators who would shape the nation's intellectual landscape.

Upon completing his rigorous training with distinction, my father returned to Ado-Ekiti to begin his career as a teacher. He dedicated himself to the profession, earning a reputation for diligence, excellence, and steadfast commitment to his students. In 1940, he was posted to Usi-Ekiti, a town about 42 kilometers from Ado-Ekiti. Unknown to him, this transfer was far more than a routine assignment—it was a divine arrangement. For it was in Usi-Ekiti that he would cross paths with the woman destined to be his wife, my beloved mother.

After many years of meritorious service to Ekiti land, my grandparents eventually retired and returned to Ogbomoso, where they lived out their later years in well-earned rest. Meanwhile, my father remained committed to his teaching career, pouring his heart into educating young minds. His influence, shaped by the discipline and values instilled in him by Grandpa and Grandma Idowu, laid the foundation for the principles that would guide my own life.

MATERNAL ANCESTRY

On my mother's side, my grandparents were proud natives of Usi-Ekiti, where they spent most of their lives deeply rooted in faith and community service. They were not just respected elders but also the spiritual pillars of their Anglican church, holding the esteemed titles of *Baba Ijo* (Father of the Church) and *Iya Ijo* (Mother of the Church). Their dedication to the church was remarkable—they led prayer meetings, actively participated in fellowships, and played key roles in organizing major church events. Their faith was both a personal conviction and a guiding force that shaped the lives of those around them, including their children and grandchildren.

My mother grew up in this environment, surrounded by discipline, faith, and a strong sense of duty. She excelled in her education, attending various teachers' training institutions to acquire the skills and qualifications needed to pursue a career in teaching. She also attended the then Women's School of Home Economics in Ekiti, where she learned valuable skills in household management, nutrition, culinary arts, child care, and various crafts. Eventually, she secured a teaching position at an Anglican school in Usi-Ekiti.

It was there that destiny brought her and my father together, leading to a love story built on shared values, mutual respect, and a deep commitment to education and faith.

With the blessings of both families, my parents were joined in marriage and soon embarked on their journey together. Not long after, they moved to Ado-Ekiti, where my father served as the principal of the renowned Christ's School. Originally founded as Ekiti Central School in 1933 by Archdeacon Henry Dallimore, Christ's School was one of the most prestigious educational institutions in the region.

Meanwhile, my mother continued to make an impact in the educational sector, teaching at Emmanuel Anglican Primary School, the oldest primary school in Ado-Ekiti. Their union was thus not just a marriage but a partnership defined by love, faith, and a shared vision for the future. Their ability to uplift and support each other through life's journey left a lasting impression on me, one that I would later carry into my own family.

TRANSGENERATIONAL IMPARTATIONS

One of the blessings of my early years was the opportunity to know and receive the care and prayers of all my grandparents before they passed away. My first encounter with my maternal grandparents was in the late 1940s when we visited their home in Usi-Ekiti. Even as a young child, I could feel their warmth and affection. They lavished us with love, constantly engaging with us, teaching us important lessons, and treating us to delicious home-cooked meals. Their nurturing presence made that visit a treasured memory that has stayed with me through the years.

A few years later, I had a similar experience with my paternal grandparents when we relocated to Ogbomoso in 1950 and briefly stayed with them. Unlike my short visit to Usi-Ekiti, this stay was longer and had an even greater impact on me. My grandparents' home in Ogbomoso was a traditional extended-family compound, bustling with relatives all living together in a tightly knit community. In that environment, love was abundant, discipline was firm, and cultural and spiritual values were passed down through generations.

Looking back, I realize how deeply my grandparents influenced the person I have become. Their lifestyles of faith, resilience, and commitment to family, which were instilled in my parents, ultimately became the bedrock upon which I built my own family. Their legacy of love, discipline, and faith continues through me, my children, and even my grandchildren, ensuring that their influence endures for generations to come.

A SISTER LIKE A MOTHER

Beyond the nurturing presence of my parents and grandparents, there was another person who played an instrumental role in shaping my formative years—my elder sister, Kikelomo (later known as Mrs. Kikelomo Ayandipo). More than just a sibling, she was like a second mother to me. Being significantly older and deeply affectionate, she took it upon herself to ensure my well-being, showering me with the kind of love, care, and protection that only a devoted big sister could provide. The fact that I was the only boy among my siblings made her even more attentive to me. She was my guardian, my protector, and my regular source of comfort.

As I grew older, I came to admire Sister Kikelomo not just for her warmth and kindness but also for her brilliance and impeccable sense of style. She was a highly intelligent woman who pursued her education in Economics at the London Polytechnic (now the University of Westminster). Her academic journey broadened her worldview, and she carried herself with a blend of sophistication and grace that made her stand out wherever she went.

Upon completing her studies, she married Barrister Oladunni Ayandipo, a distinguished lawyer, and together, they settled in Ibadan, Oyo State, after returning from London in 1971. As the years went by, Kikelomo became a prominent figure in social circles, particularly when her husband became a top-ranking political appointee in the mid-1980s. Despite the prestige and societal recognition that came with their status, she remained humble, dedicated to her career, and committed to the values she had always upheld. She had a successful career as an educator at the University of Ibadan, where she imparted knowledge to countless students until her eventual retirement.

Sadly, we lost her in 2016, but her impact remains deeply etched in my heart. The bond we shared in our childhood laid the foundation for a lifetime of sibling love, unity, and mutual support. Watching how she cared for us taught me and my younger siblings invaluable lessons about family—lessons that extended beyond childhood and have continued into our adult lives.

Growing up under her influence, we cultivated a home environment filled with love, cooperation, and friendship. We played together, shared responsibilities, supported one another, and looked out for each other in every possible way. To this day, that spirit of unity and affection continues within our family, a lasting reflection of the values she helped instill in us.

EARLIEST FRIENDSHIP

Outside of my family circle, another person whose delightful presence in my early years remains indelible in my memory was Remi Osanyi. Remi was my favorite playmate. Our families were next-door neighbors, and since we were about the same age, forming a bond was effortless. We became inseparable, spending our days in endless play, exploring the school compound where we lived, and creating adventures only children could dream up.

Remi and I were always on the move, running around with boundless energy, playing with animated toys, and making the most of our little world. Our parents, recognizing our close friendship, added an extra layer of excitement to our playtime by buying us a pair of children's tricycles. Those tricycles became our prized possessions, turning our play into grand adventures. We rode them tirelessly, pretending to transport ourselves from one imaginary destination to another, navigating the school compound as if it were an entire city. The sheer thrill of riding those toy cycles remains etched in my memory to this day.

Those early experiences with the tricycles sparked in me a fascination with automobiles. Even as a young boy, I felt an urge to one day own a real vehicle, to experience the freedom and exhilaration that driving could bring.

Looking back, my friendship with Remi was one of the highlights of my early years in Ado-Ekiti. It was a time of innocence and unfiltered joy, a time when the biggest concerns revolved around how fast we could pedal or whose tricycle could get to the imaginary finish line first. But like all childhood seasons, it eventually came to an end. In 1950, when my family moved to Ogbomoso, I had to part ways with my first best friend. Though we were too young to truly grasp the weight of goodbyes, the memories of those carefree days have delighted me since then.

3
EDUCATIONAL FOUNDATIONS

At the tender age of five, I was enrolled in Anglican Primary School in Ado-Ekiti, marking the beginning of my formal education. However, in 1950, my father made the decision to relocate our family back to our ancestral hometown, Ogbomoso. Though I was too young to fully understand the reasons behind this move, it turned out to be a well-timed decision, as both my parents quickly secured stable employment. My father was appointed as an Education Officer by the Oyo State government, while my mother took up a teaching position at St. David's Anglican School in Agboin, a historic institution founded in 1854. It was at this renowned school that I resumed and eventually completed my elementary education.

As I mentioned in the previous chapter, our initial years in Ogbomoso were spent in my paternal grandfather, Baba Agba Idowu's, sprawling compound, where we were surrounded by the warmth and care of extended family. This loving environment played a crucial role in helping me adapt seamlessly to our new life and school. The transition, which might have been daunting for some children, felt effortless for me because I was embraced by a community that valued education, discipline, and familial support.

From the very start, I enjoyed every aspect of my schooling experience. Learning came naturally to me, and I eagerly absorbed both academic subjects and extracurricular activities. My enthusiasm was particularly evident in my love for music, which was largely influenced by my father. Before completing my elementary education, I had already mastered several musical instruments, including the flute, drums, and piano.

Under my father's guidance and the school's encouragement, my musical abilities flourished. I practiced relentlessly, honing my skills until I became one of the best young musicians in the school.

Eventually, I was honored with the leadership of the school band, a position that filled my parents with immense pride.

A NEW PHASE OF LIFE

After completing elementary school, I gained admission into Ogbomoso Grammar School, Paku, in 1958. This marked a turning point in my life, as it was my first experience living away from my family in a boarding school. The transition was anything but easy. Beyond the emotional challenge of parting with my parents and siblings, I had to quickly adapt to an entirely new way of life, governed by strict rules, structured routines, and an unfamiliar social hierarchy.

Established in 1952 through the dedicated efforts of Ogbomoso Parapo—a socio-cultural organization of prominent Ogbomoso indigenes, Ogbomoso Grammar School, was then a boys-only school. The school operated with three boarding houses: Eyo Ita House, Gesinde House, and Oyerinde House. These houses were named after individuals who played crucial roles in the school's inception.

Prof. Eyo Ita, a respected educationist and the first Premier of Nigeria's Eastern Region (1951–1953), had envisioned building a university at Paku and had begun constructing a massive structure. With about half of the project completed, the building was repurposed to serve the new Grammar School's needs, housing classrooms, a boarding facility, an assembly hall, a chapel, a dining area, and quarters for the housemaster.

Chief Edmund Godwin Oluwemimo Gesinde was the school's pioneering principal, who led the institution with distinction from its inception in 1952 until 1972. Professor Nathaniel Durojaye Oyerinde not only played a crucial role in the school's founding, but also served for many years as chairman of its Board of Governors.

LEARNING TO ADAPT

Typically, students were randomly assigned to one of the three boarding houses. However, I was specifically placed in Eyo Ita House because the housemaster was from my mother's hometown. The decision was made to ensure I had a familiar guardian figure within the school system. However, as I stated above, despite this arrangement, my first few weeks were challenging.

Boarding school had a rigid hierarchy, with multiple layers of authority: the room head, the student house prefect, the housemaster, and finally, the school principal, who was the ultimate figure of discipline. Any of these authorities could issue instructions—or disciplinary actions—at any time.

At first, I found these rigid structures overwhelming, but over time, I learned to adjust to them. Gradually, boarding school taught me independence, self-discipline, and the importance of living harmoniously with peers from different backgrounds. The daily routines—waking up at dawn, adhering to strict study hours, participating in communal chores, and maintaining personal discipline—instilled values that would serve me well throughout life. I learned obedience, neatness, orderliness and unity.

Beyond the physical and social adjustments, boarding school also provided ample opportunity for my spiritual growth. The chapel assembly was an integral part of our daily routine, and Sunday services were a time of deep reflection and connection. These experiences deepened the foundation of my faith and further helped to shape my moral compass.

THRIVING AND SOARING

As I settled into the rhythm of boarding school life, I began to flourish academically and socially. I developed a special love for Mathematics, Geography, and Yoruba Language, thanks to the engaging and practical teaching style of teachers like Mr. Ayo Adelowo. Their ability to bring subjects to life made learning enjoyable and deeply impactful. I also enjoyed inter-house competitions, such as soccer, debates, wrestling and others.

Beyond academics and competitive activities, one of the greatest gifts I received from my time at Ogbomoso Grammar School was the opportunity to form deep and lasting bonds with classmates who would later play significant roles in my life. Among them was Ayodele (later Dr. Ayodele) Ayandipo of blessed memory, who became my closest companion. His older brother would eventually marry my sister, Kikelomo.

Though I was a year ahead of Ayodele, we were inseparable. We shared everything—from school supplies to personal belongings—and even dressed alike, leading many to assume we were twins. Whether in school or back home during the holidays, we remained by each other's side from 1959 until our graduation.

I also shared close friendships with Fasasi (later Dr. Fasasi) Aminu and Joe Adeyemo (both of blessed memory), as well as Demola Ayanlowo and Dimeji Ogunjumo. Looking back, I can't help but marvel at how divine orchestration seemed to place these individuals in my life at such a formative stage. Each of them, in one way or another, contributed to shaping me into the person I would become.

MEETING MY FUTURE WIFE

One of the most cherished memories from my secondary school years unfolded quite unexpectedly in 1960, when I was in Form 3. That year, my father received a transfer posting to Sapele, in present-day Delta State. By this time, our family had grown weary of constantly uprooting our lives to follow his numerous transfers, so we made a collective decision to remain in Ogbomoso, where we had already established a stable and thriving life.

As fate would have it, my father's longtime friend, Justice Olayinka Odumosu, was also transferred to

Sapele as a High Court Judge. This coincidence was a source of great joy for both men, whose friendship spanned decades.

To provide some background, my father and Justice Odumosu first met as students at St. Andrew's College, Oyo, where they forged a deep and lasting friendship. Later, both of them secured teaching positions at Christ's School, Ado-Ekiti, further solidifying their bond and intertwining the lives of their families.

With both men now stationed far away in Sapele, it was only natural that their families would make plans to visit them during the long school holiday. That singular trip would change the course of my life forever.

It was during that visit that I met Olawunmi, the brilliant and captivating daughter of Justice Odumosu. She was in Form 1 at the time, and though she was younger, her bubbly personality, intelligence, and effortless charm made an unforgettable impression on me. She carried herself with a rare combination of liveliness and grace, crowned with a beauty that was simply mesmerizing.

Almost instantly, we struck up a friendship, and the more time we spent together, the more our bond deepened. The holiday in Sapele was one of the most memorable of my youth—not just because of the new experiences and adventures it brought, but because of the quiet, unspoken spark that began to grow between Wunmi and me.

At the time, neither of us could have foreseen the journey that spark would take us on—how it would evolve into a beautiful love story, one that would endure for many years and later blossom into a blissful marriage.

GODSENT GUIDES FROM AMERICA

The most defining moment in my time at Ogbomoso Grammar School came in 1961, when members of the American Peace Corps arrived at our school. Their presence would leave an indelible mark on my educational journey, shaping my ambitions in ways I never anticipated.

The Peace Corps had been established by President John F. Kennedy on March 1, 1961, through an executive order. Its mission was to promote world peace and friendship by sending American volunteers to developing nations, where they would assist in key areas such as education, healthcare, and community development.

Across the countries where they were stationed, these volunteers helped strengthen local education systems, improve literacy rates, modernize teaching methods, and introduce innovative learning techniques. Nigeria was one of the many countries that benefited immensely from their work, particularly in the education sector.

When they arrived at Ogbomoso Grammar School, their impact was immediate and immense. They specialized in subjects like English, Science, and Mathematics, and their expertise transformed the way we learned. Unlike the traditional rote learning methods that had been common, these volunteers brought a more practical, engaging, and student-centered approach to teaching.

I still vividly remember Rev. Earl Fine, who taught us the principles of Physics (as part of our General Science subject) with such clarity and enthusiasm that the subject, which many found daunting, suddenly became exciting and comprehensible. He connected physics concepts to real-life applications in industry and daily life, often referencing insights from the U.S. Science Academy to inspire us.

Similarly, Mr. Tudor, our Mathematics teacher, introduced us to modern problem-solving techniques that made even the most complex equations seem approachable. His methods transformed the way I saw numbers, deepening my love for analytical thinking.

But the influence of the Peace Corps volunteers extended far beyond academic engagements. They encouraged us to think critically, question assumptions, and engage actively in learning. Their involvement in debating clubs, drama, and sports injected new energy into our extracurricular activities, making school life more dynamic and enriching.

Their presence also reinforced our Christian values and spiritual growth. Many of them participated in our chapel services, moral instruction, and mentorship programs. I recall how volunteers from the Southern Baptist Convention often preached in our school chapel and even invited students to their homes for dinner, creating a sense of warmth and encouragement that strengthened our faith.

DREAMING BIG

The professionalism, kindness, and dedication of the Peace Corps volunteers left a such a lasting impression on me that I began to nurture the burning aspiration of studying in the United States. I was firmly convinced that my future lay in studying abroad. I was particularly drawn to two fields: Civil Engineering and Geology.

My passion for these courses was deeply influenced by two role models—my uncle, Engineer Idowu (of blessed memory), who was a civil engineer, and Chief Tunde Aluko, a geologist working for Gulf Oil. I greatly admired the works of these two men. Their technical expertise, problem-solving skills, and hands-on approach to engineering and exploration fascinated me. I was especially drawn to the thrill of field operations, the excitement of overseas assignments, and the vast possibilities that these careers presented.

My heart was set. I dreamed of following in their footsteps and making a meaningful impact in my chosen profession. However, just as this ambition began to consume my thoughts, two major challenges arose—challenges that threatened to derail my dreams and made me question whether I was merely chasing a mirage.

THE "PER ARDUA" FACTOR

A fundamental philosophy that shaped the education and training we received at Ogbomoso Grammar School was embodied in the school's official motto: "Per ardua ad astra". This Latin phrase, proudly displayed on our school badges and blazer jackets, translates to "Through difficulties to the stars." It was a principle ingrained in us by our principal and teachers to serve as a constant reminder that success was not handed out freely but earned through perseverance and resilience.

Essentially, we were trained to understand that life would not be a smooth ride, but with determination and hard work, we could overcome any obstacle and reach the heights of achievement. This echoes the words of Psalm 66:12: *"You have caused men to ride over our heads; We went through fire and through water; But You brought us out to rich fulfillment."*

However, for someone like me, who had enjoyed a relatively smooth and fulfilling childhood, the full weight of this philosophy did not immediately resonate. While I understood the value of discipline and diligence, I had yet to face any significant challenges that could make the school's motto truly personal. That all changed when I began to realize that my academic and career dreams were in jeopardy.

MAJOR LIMITATION

To start with, Ogbomoso Grammar School, being a local government institution, lacked a full science curriculum. Due to financial constraints, the school did not have the necessary laboratory facilities or teachers to offer core science subjects. At the time, only General Science and Health Science were available as part of the School Certificate/General Certificate Examinations (SCE/GCE). It was not until 1965—three years after my graduation—that Physics, Chemistry, and Biology were introduced as separate subjects.

This limitation was devastating for me. As I revealed earlier, my ambition was to pursue a career in Civil Engineering or Geology, both of which required strong foundations in Mathematics, Physics, and Chemistry. Without those subjects, my secondary school certificate was inadequate for university admission into the sciences. The realization hit me hard, leaving me anxious about my future.

However, despite my concerns, I refused to be discouraged. I remained focused on my studies, determined to excel in the subjects available to me. When I sat for my final exams in 1962, I achieved excellent results. But even as I celebrated my results, a more pressing question loomed: *What next?*

PRE-UNIVERSITY STRUGGLES

With my secondary school education behind me, I found myself stuck in a frustrating predicament. My certificate, though strong in other areas, lacked the science credentials necessary to pursue my dream career. I knew I needed an alternative route, but I wasn't sure where to start.

Fortunately, As I sought advice from friends and mentors, I learned about the Federal Emergency Science School in Onikan, Lagos. The moment I learned about it, I knew this was the solution I had been looking for.

Established in 1960, the Federal Emergency Science School was part of Nigeria's post-independence strategy to rapidly develop a workforce in science and technology. At the time, the country was grappling with a critical shortage of scientists, engineers, and medical professionals. To address this, the government set up specialized emergency science schools across Nigeria to train students in core scientific disciplines.

The Lagos institution was one of several emergency science schools set up across the country, offering intensive remedial programs for students who, like me, had not received adequate training in the sciences during their secondary education. The curriculum was rigorous, covering core subjects such as Mathematics, Physics, Chemistry, and Biology. The goal was to equip students with the necessary qualifications to compete for university admission in highly specialized fields, including Medicine, Engineering, and the pure sciences. Upon successful completion of the two-year program, students were awarded the General Certificate in Education (GCE) in science subjects, making them eligible for higher studies.

This was exactly what I needed. The thought of finally gaining the science education required for my chosen field filled me with excitement and renewed determination. But as quickly as my hopes were rekindled, another obstacle emerged—finances.

By this time, my family's financial situation was stretched thin. With my younger sisters advancing through secondary school and my parents already struggling with household expenses, there simply wasn't enough money to support my additional education. My older sister, still trying to find her footing in life, was also unable to help.

For a moment, it felt as if my dream was slipping away before it even had the chance to take flight. The financial burden was real, and the path forward was uncertain. But if there was one thing I had learned from my parents, my school, and my own experiences, it was this: *You never give up on your future.*

The lessons of perseverance echoed in my mind. *Per ardua ad astra.* If success required hardship, then I was prepared to fight for it. I resolved that no matter how difficult the journey, I would not give up.

Thus, with nothing but my determination and the small amount my parents could afford to give me, I set out for Lagos in 1963—ready to face whatever challenges lay ahead.

FROM CALM TO CHAOS

Leaving behind my family and the serene, familiar township of Ogbomoso to start a new life in Lagos— the then capital of Nigeria—was a daunting transition. Though I was captivated by the towering buildings, bustling streets, and vibrant energy of the city, I was equally overwhelmed by its sheer size, relentless movement, and seeming disorder.

The Lagos I encountered was a world away from the quiet rhythm of Ogbomoso. The city never seemed to rest; it pulsed with activity at all hours, and its crowded streets, blaring vehicle horns, and the ceaseless chatter of street vendors left me in a state of culture shock.

I moved in with my cousin, Mr. Yaya Balogun (of blessed memory), who shared a small single-room rented unit with a friend in the densely populated Ebute-Metta area of Lagos Mainland. Unlike the spacious, open environment I had known back home, I now found myself navigating a congested neighborhood where privacy was a luxury and noise was constant. Life here was far from easy, but I remained focused on my goal of completing my remedial science program at the Federal Emergency Science School.

To sustain myself financially, I took on a part-time job as a third-class clerk at the Federal Ministry of Foreign Affairs in Marina, Lagos. Juggling work and studies was not easy, but I was determined to persevere. Each day was a test of endurance—long commutes, demanding coursework, and the relentless grind of city life. But against all odds, I successfully completed the remedial science program, taking one step closer to my dream of pursuing higher education.

THE HSC CHALLENGE

With the remedial program behind me, the next academic hurdle was obtaining the Higher School Certificate (HSC), a critical qualification for university admission at the time. Before the establishment of the Joint Admissions and Matriculation Board (JAMB) in 1978, students aspiring to study competitive courses such as Engineering, Medicine, and Law—or those aiming for admission into Nigeria's most prestigious universities—were required to complete the HSC program. This two-year pre-university curriculum, modeled after the British educational system, involved intensive study in three principal subjects and one subsidiary subject, depending on the student's intended course of study. The final examinations were conducted by the West African Examinations Council (WAEC) or the Cambridge University Examination Board, and successful candidates were eligible for direct entry into university, often at an advanced level.

Initially, I planned to remain in Lagos for the HSC program, believing that studying in the bustling metropolis would present more opportunities. However, reality quickly set in. The high cost of living, coupled with the exhausting and chaotic environment, became increasingly difficult to manage. The daily grind of city life, once exhilarating, soon became a burden. Lagos demanded relentless energy, and as much as I tried, I found myself struggling to keep up.

Eventually, I reached a breaking point. The financial strain, coupled with the overwhelming nature of the city, forced me to reconsider my options. Reluctantly, I decided to return to Ogbomoso. Yet, despite my departure from Lagos, my resolve to pursue higher education remained unshaken. I knew I had to find another way forward.

As fate would have it, a timely conversation with my secondary school friend, Dimeji Ogunjumo, led me to a new opportunity. Dimeji was preparing to begin his HSC program at Olivet Baptist High School (formerly Oyo Baptist Boys' High School) in Oyo. He spoke enthusiastically about the school's strong academic reputation, particularly its robust science curriculum, well-equipped laboratories, and an impressive track record of student success in science subjects. His glowing recommendation intrigued me, and after careful consideration, I decided to follow in his footsteps.

In 1965, I moved to Oyo to enroll at Olivet Baptist High School, making arrangements to stay with a friend, Henry Oladele (of blessed memory). From the moment I arrived, I knew I had made the right choice. The school's structured learning environment, coupled with its affiliation with the Baptist mission, bore a striking resemblance to the American education system. More interestingly, a significant number of American Peace Corps volunteers served as teachers and mentors, providing not only academic guidance but also spiritual and personal development. Their presence reminded me of my secondary school days, where I had benefitted immensely from similar influences.

Beyond academics, my stay in Oyo was made significantly easier by Henry's generosity. Understanding my financial constraints, he volunteered to subsidize my feeding and transportation costs, easing my burden tremendously. This act of kindness allowed me to concentrate fully on my studies without the constant worry of making ends meet. With renewed determination and a more conducive learning environment, I threw myself wholeheartedly into my studies, determined to excel in the HSC program.

5
MY AMERICAN VISA MIRACLE

After successfully earning my Higher School Certificate (HSC) in 1967, I secured admission that same year to study Civil Engineering at the prestigious University of Lagos (UNILAG), Akoka. Given my family's financial situation, I knew that pursuing my dream of studying in the United States was out of the question. It wasn't just unrealistic—it was unthinkable. So, I didn't even attempt to chase that dream. Instead, I focused on the opportunity before me and embraced my new reality at UNILAG.

But then, even paying for the UNILAG program was another challenge in itself. I scraped together funds from my parents, relatives, and friends just to afford the fees for my first year. Once I managed to get through that hurdle, I threw myself into the rhythms of campus life. From attending lectures, to completing assignments, participating in practicals, and enjoying the social aspects of university life, I tried to make the best of my time at UNILAG.

I have to admit that, despite the financial strain constantly looming over me, I had many moments of joy at UNILAG. I was assigned to Hollywood Hostel, located next to the Lagos State College of Education Chapel at the time. My roommate, Bode Osunsanmi, came from a similarly cash-strapped background, which made it easier for us to bond. We understood each other's struggles and found solace in our friendship, lifting each other's spirits through the highs and lows of university life.

One of the highlights of my time at UNILAG was the quality of the lectures and the brilliance of the lecturers. I particularly remember Professor Ayo Awojobi (of blessed memory), who taught us both Engineering Mathematics and Engineering Design & Drawing. He had the rare gift of making complex subjects simple, engaging, and accessible. His teaching style inspired me and made me appreciate engineering even more.

A DREAM CUT SHORT

Soon, however, my biggest fear became reality. After struggling to pay for my first year, the burden of tuition became too great. There was no financial aid or student loan system to turn to, and despite my relentless efforts to find a part-time job, nothing worked out. By 1969, I had exhausted every possible avenue for funding, and the university had run out of patience. I was asked to withdraw.

The blow was devastating. I had worked so hard to get into university, only to be forced out, not because of poor performance but because of money. My roommate, Bode, suffered the same fate.

The experience left me both heartbroken and furious. How could a nation fail its students so badly? How could there be no system in place to support eager, intelligent young minds who wanted nothing more than to learn and contribute to society? Especially in a field as critical as engineering?

From that moment, one thing became clear—I had to leave Nigeria. If the system had no place for me, I would find a place elsewhere. Bode felt the same way, and together, we resolved to do whatever it took to legally migrate to America.

CHASING THE AMERICAN DREAM

I moved back in with my uncle, Yahya Balogun, in the Ebute-Metta area of Lagos, and my desperation to leave Nigeria intensified. I was determined to secure an American visa. I sought advice from different people, but the responses were overwhelmingly discouraging. Most people told me I was wasting my time.

"You don't have financial sponsorship," they reminded me over and over again. "Without proof of funding, you don't stand a chance."

The warnings didn't deter me. I knew America had opportunities waiting for me, and I refused to believe there wasn't a way in. Something deep inside me told me to keep pushing forward—to exhaust every possibility. That instinct became my driving force.

Two of my secondary school friends that I mentioned earlier were Joe Adeyemo and Fasasi Aminu (both of blessed memory). We all shared same views, one of which was the dream of travelling to the United States for our university education. By this time, their dream had been fulfilled – Joe was studying at the University of Chicago, Illinois; while Fasasi was at the University of Oregon, Eugene.

I reached out to these friends and explained my predicament. They assured me that there were plenty of academic opportunities in their respective states. They also advised that instead of applying for a student visa, I should apply for a visiting visa, which might be easier to obtain and could later be converted into a student visa. Even then, they warned that I would still need to prove some level of financial stability.

By this time, I had secured a temporary job with Nigerian Telecommunications. It wasn't much, but it was something. Clinging to that small thread of hope, I decided to apply for a visitor visa.

THE MIRACULOUS BREAKTHROUGH

On the day of my visa interview, I arrived at the U.S. Embassy with a mix of determination and nerves. I had mentally prepared myself for a barrage of questions about my financial status, my long-term plans, and why I wasn't applying for a student visa instead. I braced myself, ready to make the best case I could.

Then, the unexpected happened.

The interviewer asked me a question: "What are you doing at the moment?"

I replied truthfully, explaining that I had recently left an engineering program at UNILAG and was temporarily working a vacation job. I added that I wanted to visit the United States.

To my absolute shock, the interviewer didn't ask for financial proof. No grilling, no skepticism—nothing. He simply nodded, approved my visa, and told me to return in a few days to pick it up.

I walked out of that embassy in disbelief. I had prepared for every possible challenge, every argument I might need to make—and yet, the process had gone so smoothly, proving that divine intervention was at work!

AMERICA, HERE I COME

With my American visa finally in my hands, I was overwhelmed with joy. It felt like I had conquered the impossible, like I was standing at the threshold of a brand-new destiny. But even as my heart swelled with excitement, I knew the journey was far from over. The visa was only the key—the door still had to be pushed open. There were travel expenses to cover, the most pressing of which was the flight ticket. Without that, my American dream would remain just that—a dream.

Once again, my friends in the United States came through for me. Joe, in particular, extended an extraordinary gesture of kindness. He arranged a loaned flight ticket for me that would take me straight to Chicago, Illinois. The understanding was that once I secured my first job, I would repay the cost of the ticket. That act of generosity lifted a huge weight off my shoulders.

With my biggest expense taken care of, I pulled together every available resource. I gathered my modest savings, received contributions from family and well-wishers, and carefully assembled the few essentials I could afford for the journey. I wasn't traveling in luxury, but I was traveling with purpose.

Then came the moment that would change my life forever. On a beautiful day in August 1970, I boarded a Swiss Air flight from Lagos. Seventeen hours later, I stepped onto American soil for the very first time, with just a luggage box and less than $250!

Indeed, no words can truly capture the euphoria that filled my heart the moment I landed in Chicago. It was as though time itself paused to acknowledge this monumental moment in my life. Just months before, this had seemed like an impossible fantasy—something too far-fetched to even pursue. And yet, here I was, standing in the land of limitless possibilities.

The weight of past disappointments melted away in that instant. The pain of being forced to withdraw from UNILAG, the crushing frustration of Nigeria's rigid educational system, the struggle to secure a visa—all of it had led me to this very moment. What had once felt like a cruel setback had become an open door to greater opportunities.

Later on, I received even more incredible news—Bode Osunsanmi, my dear friend and partner in struggle, had also made it! He, too, had overcome the same challenges, secured his visa, and arrived in New York around the same time I did. What a moment of divine orchestration! The same education system that had shut us out had unknowingly propelled us toward a far greater future. *Hallelujah!*

LESSONS FROM THE JOURNEY

One paramount lesson I learned from that visa episode and my relocation to America is that success is never just about talent or intelligence—it is about resolute determination, persistence, and the willingness to make sacrifices for a greater goal. It is about recognizing when to press forward despite obstacles and when to humbly accept help from those who genuinely care.

But more than anything, my journey to America was a powerful proof of God's unfailing purpose for my life. By all human logic, I should never have been granted that visa. The odds were stacked against me. Financial evidence was the most crucial requirement at the time, and I had none. But where logic failed, grace prevailed.

I now see clearly that God destined me to leave Nigeria and fulfill my purpose in the United States. Every hardship, every disappointment, every impossible situation was simply a stepping stone to something greater. Philippians 4:13 sums up my story perfectly:

"I can do all things through Christ who strengthens me."

From my experience, that verse applies to every area of life, including the economic and personal challenges we face. Through Christ, we are empowered to rise above obstacles, break limitations, and walk boldly into the future He has prepared for us!

6
REALITIES OF AN IMMIGRANT

Having a great friend like Joe Adeyemo already settled in Chicago was a major advantage for me when I arrived there. It meant that I had a place to stay, a guide to help me navigate my new reality, and a sense of familiarity in an otherwise foreign land. As planned, I moved into the small two-bedroom apartment he shared with another roommate on 63rd Street, near Champlain Avenue and Martin Luther King Drive, in the heart of Chicago's South Side.

Let me quickly state that the Chicago I stepped into was a city bustling with life and industry; but beneath its thriving surface were deep social fractures. It was a major manufacturing hub, with steel mills and industrial plants shaping its skyline, but the economic tides were shifting. Factory closures were leaving thousands unemployed, and entire neighborhoods—especially in the South Side—were sinking into poverty and crime.

The streets were simply restless. Violent crime was on the rise, with homicides, armed robberies, and drug-related offenses becoming an everyday reality. Gangs ruled certain blocks, and territorial disputes often turned deadly. Racial tensions simmered just beneath the surface, sometimes erupting into open conflict.

The police presence in these neighborhoods was inconsistent, either too harsh or alarmingly absent. Also, while activist groups like the Black Panthers were passionately fighting for justice, they were also adding to the atmosphere of unrest. Adding to the chaos was a worsening heroin epidemic, which gripped the community in ways I had never seen before.

It was apparent therefore that, for a newcomer like me, survival in such an environment not only required caution but also demanded strong adaptability skills. Joe and his roommate supported me in achieving this. They taught me how to move wisely, when to speak and when to stay silent, and which streets to avoid at certain hours. I quickly learned that blending in was my best strategy.

A GREATER BATTLE

Despite the volatility of my new neighborhood, I managed to avoid trouble. But there was one battle I simply could not win—the brutal Chicago weather.

To make ends meet and repay my debt to Joe for the flight ticket, I had secured a night-shift job at a metal fabrication company, grinding flat metal saws. The work was backbreaking—long hours of repetitive motion, ears ringing from the deafening machinery, and the ever-present risk of injury from flying sparks and metal dust. The factory floor was a brutal environment, demanding precision, endurance, and sheer willpower.

Yet, I took it all in stride. I was no stranger to hard work. The need to survive, earn a living, and secure my future overshadowed any complaints I might have had about the exhausting nature of the job. But one thing I hadn't accounted for was the sheer brutality of a Chicago winter. The wind that swept through the city wasn't just cold but also was piercing, cutting through layers of clothing as if they weren't even there. Temperatures often plunged well below freezing, sometimes as low as -20°F (-29°C), with wind chills that made it feel even worse. Snowstorms turned streets into ice traps, and the daily battle of commuting to work became almost unbearable.

I had never experienced anything like it. Back home in Nigeria, the weather was predictable—warm and humid, with seasonal rains. But here, I found myself walking to bus stops in the dead of night, my breath turning to ice in the air, my fingers numb despite my gloves. The cold crept into my bones, and before long, it began to take a serious toll on my health. My joints ached terribly, searing arthritic pains that made even the simplest movements agonizing.

The irony wasn't lost on me: I had come all this way in search of opportunity, only to find that my greatest struggle wasn't the job, the crime, or the culture shock—but simply enduring the cold.

MASSIVE RESPITE

For nearly a year, I endured Chicago's merciless weather, driven by the need to repay my debts and stay financially afloat. However, as the Yoruba saying goes,

"When you stay silent, your affliction silently kills you." As the biting cold gnawed at my bones and the relentless arthritic pain grew unbearable, I realized I desperately needed to seek a way out. That was when I reached out to my other good friend, Dr. Fasasi Aminu, who was then a graduate student in the Department of Architecture at the University of Oregon.

When I shared my struggles with Fasasi, he was very understanding. He knew firsthand how challenging it was to adapt to a new country, and he sympathized with my plight. Without hesitation, he encouraged me to consider relocating to Oregon, assuring me that the weather was far more tolerable than Chicago's unforgiving winters. More importantly, he informed me that the University of Oregon offered better financial aid opportunities for students, which could significantly ease my financial burden.

I didn't need much convincing. The promise of relief from the unforgiving cold and a better financial support system was too good to ignore. Following Fasasi's advice, I quickly gathered my documents and submitted my application to the University of Oregon. Fortunately, I had already managed to convert my visiting visa into a student visa, which made the process significantly smoother.

Later that same year, in 1971, I received an official offer of admission to pursue a Bachelor of Science degree in Geology at the University of Oregon. The sheer joy that flooded my heart in that moment was indescribable. After everything I had been through—the heartbreak of leaving UNILAG, the struggle to get to America, the grueling work in the factory, the cold-induced arthritis nightmare—this moment felt nothing short of a divine intervention.

That offer was, for me, a second chance, a lifeline, a fresh start. Not only was I escaping the brutal Chicago winters and the volatility of the South Side, but I was also reclaiming my academic dreams. As I mentioned earlier, Geology had always been one of my dream career paths, and now, against all odds, I had another opportunity to pursue it.

Interestingly, the news of my admission not only excited me but also inspired Joe. Despite being in Chicago before me, he, too, had long endured the city's punishing winters and the rising cost of living.

Seeing my breakthrough ignited something in him. My success became his motivation, and before long, he also applied for a transfer to the University of Oregon.

The following year, Joe joined Fasasi and me in Oregon. It was like stepping back in time, as we rekindled our close-knit friendship from our secondary school days and relived those cherished memories together.

LIFE AT UNIVERSITY OF OREGON, EUGENE

I arrived in Eugene, Oregon, in August 1971 to begin my Bachelor of Science degree in Geology with about $2,000 in savings, after having fully repaid the loan for my flight ticket from Nigeria. Leaving behind the brutal cold and tough living conditions of Chicago's South Side, I found Eugene to be a refreshing change—a city with mild, rainy weather, a lower cost of living, and a far more welcoming atmosphere for international students.

The people of Eugene were friendly, and the general environment was accommodating, making my transition much smoother than I had anticipated. But beyond the generally genial atmosphere, what made my transition to life in Oregon so easy was the International Friends Program, an initiative designed by the university to connect foreign students with local American families. The goal was to foster cross-cultural understanding, provide a sense of belonging, and help students adjust to life in the United States.

Each international student was paired with a "friendship family", based on mutual interests and compatibility. I was paired with Mr. and Mrs. Carl Web (of blessed memory), a warm and generous retired couple who welcomed me into their lives like family. They invited me for meals, celebrated my birthday with Nigerian friends, and took me on scenic road trips across Oregon. Their kindness helped me integrate into American society, understand the culture better, and feel at home despite being thousands of miles away from Nigeria.

ACADEMIC ENGAGEMENTS

The Geology Department at the University of Oregon was rigorous and well-established, having separated from the Geography Department in 1958. By the time I enrolled, it was housed in a modern science facility built in 1960, which featured well-equipped laboratories and the university's largest lecture hall. The faculty members were highly engaged in research, providing students with opportunities to participate in geological studies and fieldwork.

One of the most exciting aspects of my studies was the frequent field excursions. Nearly every weekend, we embarked on geological field trips to observe Oregon's remarkable volcanic landscapes, scenic coastlines, and unique geological formations. Some of the most unforgettable excursions included trips to Crater Lake, the Oregon Coast, and other breathtaking geological wonders. These hands-on experiences reinforced my passion for Geology and made my academic journey deeply fulfilling.

Incidentally, a major attraction that initially drew me to the University of Oregon, beyond its conducive weather and quality education, was its 50 per cent tuition discount for international students. This discount was conditional on maintaining a legal student visa and a minimum GPA of 3.0 each semester. For a foreign student like me, this was an incredible incentive—not only was it cost-effective, but it also motivated me to remain focused and committed to excelling in my studies.

SAD NEWS FROM HOME

Once I had settled in Eugene, I rented a modest studio apartment near the campus, which was typical of a university town like Eugene and relatively affordable. However, financial survival was a daily struggle, as I had little or no financial support from home. To make ends meet, I had to work full-time while juggling my academic responsibilities. The workload was demanding, but I remained determined to succeed, knowing that my education was the key to a better future.

In all, life in Eugene was fulfilling—I was excelling in my studies, surrounded by supportive friends and well-wishers, and adapting well to my new environment. However, just as I was settling into my new life and finding a rhythm, tragedy struck.

In 1972, I received devastating news from Nigeria that my beloved father had passed away after a brief illness. At the time, he had already retired and was living in Ogbomoso, enjoying the fruits of his labor. His death was a massive blow to my family, leaving behind a deep emotional and financial void.

That shocking news shattered me, not only because I had lost the man who had been our rock and anchor, but also because I never got the chance to see him again before his passing. One of my greatest dreams had been to make my father proud, to see the joy in his eyes when I graduated, and to repay his sacrifices by taking care of him in his old age. Now, all of that was gone.

For a long time, I struggled with guilt and sorrow, knowing he would never witness my academic and career successes. But despite the pain, I reminded myself of his dreams for me—he had always wanted me to excel, to rise above challenges, and to fulfill my potential.

Thus, rather than allowing grief to consume me, I resolved to keep pushing forward. If anything, his passing became an even greater motivation for me to achieve everything I had set out to do. I knew that the best way to honor his memory was to keep striving, keep conquering, and ultimately, make him proud—even if he was no longer there to see it.

7
A MIGHTY ESCAPE

As I look back on my time at the University of Oregon—and indeed, the entire journey of my life—I can joyfully say that the biggest and most consistent highlight has been the faithfulness of the Almighty God. From the very beginning, His loving hand has guided me, even when I was too preoccupied to specifically request for His help.

I say this in particular because during those undergraduate years that I've just described in the previous chapter, I was not that religious. The intense demands of combining full-time schooling with a full-time job often left me with very little time for church activities. Sundays often meant catching up on sleep, studying, or simply recovering from exhaustion. Yet, God never abandoned me. Through every situation, He was there—granting me favor, ordering my steps, shielding me from danger, and preserving me from calamities I never even saw coming.

One of such unforgettable manifestations of God's favor and protection upon me happened in 1974. At that point, I had made significant progress in my studies. Despite the financial struggles, despite the emotional toll of my father's sudden passing, and despite the countless hours spent balancing work and studies, I had pushed through.

Now, having successfully met almost all the requirements needed to graduate, one final hurdle remained before I could achieve the dream I had nurtured since 1962—the dream of earning a Geology degree. That last requirement was the Field Mapping Practical Project.

Field mapping was not just another academic exercise; it was a defining moment for every geology student. It involved physically venturing into the field, analyzing geological formations, collecting samples, and meticulously recording observations. It was a grueling, labor-intensive process that required endurance, strength, and agility. The University of Oregon placed immense importance on this project, making it a core prerequisite for graduation.

For most students, it was simply a rigorous academic challenge. For me, however, it became an unforgettable, life-threatening ordeal.

THE BEGINNING OF THE ORDEAL

A year before the field project, I had begun experiencing unusual pain and stiffness in my bones and joints. At first, I dismissed it as mere fatigue, attributing it to the stress of my daily routine. But as the days turned into weeks, the discomfort escalated into persistent, agonizing pain that made even simple tasks excruciatingly difficult.

Concerned, I visited a doctor who referred me to a rheumatologist. After several tests, I was diagnosed with rheumatoid arthritis, a chronic autoimmune condition that was already affecting all my joints and bones. The rheumatologist clearly stated that my case was severe, and the only way to manage the excruciating pain was maximum daily doses of aspirin. Even then, the medication could only offer temporary relief, not a cure. He prescribed constant rest and avoidance of strenuous activities, two recommendations that, given my full-time studies and job, seemed nearly impossible.

I tried my best to endure, hoping the condition would improve, but by the time I approached my final year field mapping project, I knew I was in trouble. This was not an ordinary academic exercise but one that required days of rigorous trekking through rough terrains, climbing rocks, carrying equipment, and working for long hours under the sun and rain. Given my deteriorating health, I knew it was physically impossible for me to complete such a task without serious consequences.

Hoping for a lifeline, I formally applied for a medical waiver to skip the field project and still qualify for graduation. To my dismay, the university administration denied my request. Instead, they suggested that I switch my major from Geology to a different, less physically demanding field.

Of course, for me, that was not an option. I had sacrificed too much, endured too many hardships, and nurtured this dream for too long to give up now. Abandoning Geology would mean surrendering the very thing I had fought for since secondary school. I had come too far to turn back. So, despite the pain, despite the warnings, despite the odds, I stood my ground—I would complete the project and graduate, no matter what it took.

In hindsight, that moment was one of the greatest tests of faith in my life. I was standing before a giant obstacle, much like the biblical David before Goliath. But just as David did not back down, I refused to retreat.

I held on to the unshakable belief that God, who had brought me this far, would see me through. As 1 John 4:4 says:

"You are of God, little children, and have overcome them, because He who is in you is greater than he who is in the world."

PRESSED BEYOND MEASURE

With my medical waiver request denied, I had no choice but to join my course mates for the mandatory field mapping project. My body protested violently, but my resolve remained unshaken. I would finish what I had started, no matter the cost.

The mapping exercise required us to spend three months in a remote base camp on Mount Ashland, the highest peak in the Siskiyou Mountains of Southern Oregon. Though it was the summer season, the mountain's 8,000-foot altitude ensured that temperatures remained frigid, with chilling winds that cut through the skin like knives. This, on its own, was an ordeal—but for me, battling rheumatoid arthritis, it became an excruciating nightmare. The cold worsened my pain, turning my joints into what felt like frozen steel, locked in agony.

Despite the hostile environment, the project had to continue. It involved three major mapping assignments, each to be conducted individually using fundamental geological mapping techniques. Each student was assigned a specific mapping block and was paired with another for tracking safety. The rule was for us to return to base camp before darkness fell.

As the days passed, the physical demands of the project became brutal. Each step on the rugged terrain sent shockwaves of pain through my bones.

Every ascent felt like a war against my own body. But I refused to give in. I clung fiercely to my ultimate goal—a Bachelor's degree in Geology—as if my very existence depended on it.

It was a time of unrelenting agony, a season I can only describe as torture. The biting cold became an enemy I could not escape. The sharp, relentless pain in my joints grew unbearable, gnawing at my endurance like a predator stalking its prey.

There were nights in the camp when I lay awake, shivering and writhing in pain, questioning if I had the strength to go on. More than once, the temptation to quit whispered to me: *"Why not just walk into the registrar's office and switch to another major? Why endure this suffering?"*

But every time the thought of quitting crossed my mind, another voice inside me roared back with defiance: *"You have come too far to turn back now!"*

Quitting would mean throwing away years of relentless effort. It would mean watching my dream slip through my fingers after fighting so hard. I refused to surrender. I chose to endure.

PER ARDUA AD ASTRA

But nothing could have prepared me for what happened next.

STRANDED BUT SAFEGUARDED

One fateful afternoon, my condition reached a breaking point.

That day, I had ventured deep into my assigned mapping block, struggling through pain but determined to complete my work. But as the hours passed, fatigue overwhelmed me. My body felt like lead, and each step became a battle. The sun began its descent, and I knew I had to start my journey back to camp before darkness fell.

But I was too slow. My legs, crippled by pain, could not carry me fast enough. The rugged terrain stretched endlessly before me, each step more painful than the last. The night arrived too quickly.

Suddenly, the forest was pitch black.

I was lost, alone, and completely stranded in the vast wilderness of the Klamath-Siskiyou region, an untamed expanse straddling the California-Oregon border. This area, spanning 11 million acres of dense wildlands, was notorious for being home to black bears and mountain lions.

I was defenseless, exhausted, and utterly vulnerable but I knew my only option was to survive the night alone in the wilderness. I stumbled upon a small clearing overshadowed by towering trees. The darkness was absolute, pressing against me like a suffocating weight. Then, in the silence of the night, I heard the distant whirring of a helicopter.

I looked up, spotting a searchlight slicing through the dense canopy of trees above me. They were looking for me!

Hope flared for a moment—only to be swiftly crushed. The helicopter circled above but could not spot me beneath the thick forest cover. Eventually, they gave up and flew away.

I was officially alone.

The night stretched on, a terrifying void of uncertainty. I could not sleep—not just because of the pain, but because we had been warned that this region was home to predators. I imagined glowing eyes watching me from the shadows, waiting for the perfect moment to strike.

To stay awake, I paced back and forth within the small clearing, my heart pounding with every rustling sound in the darkness. The cold bit into my skin, but adrenaline kept me on edge.

Two events from that night remain etched in my memory as proof of divine intervention. First, the night felt strangely short. Despite being stranded for several hours, it seemed to pass in an instant. It was as if time itself had been altered. Second, as soon as I survived the night, my journey back to camp was mysteriously swift. Immediately daylight broke and I could read my navigation compass, I miraculously found my way back to camp in just twenty minutes—a route that should have far much longer in my condition.

INCREDIBLE REUNION

When I finally walked into the camp that morning, the entire crew sat in stunned silence. Their faces were pale with shock—they had lost all hope of my survival.

One of them finally broke the silence, whispering in

disbelief: *"We thought you were gone…"*

At that moment, I realized the gravity of what had happened. I had spent an entire night alone in the wilderness, in a region known for deadly predators, with no weapon, no light, and no protection—yet, I had emerged completely unharmed.

I felt as though I had been walking in a trance the entire time, shielded by an unseen presence.

Even now, as I recall that moment, my emotions overwhelm me. The sheer reality of how close I came to death makes my heart race. But even more, the undeniable presence of God in that experience fills me with gratitude.

The truth of Psalm 23:4 comes alive in my soul: *""Even though I walk through the valley of the shadow of death, I will fear no evil, for You are with me; Your rod and Your staff, they comfort me."* Hallelujah!

Indeed, the Lord is my shepherd (Psalm 23:1), and His gracious protection is the only reason I stand today. That night should have been my last, but God had other plans.

The rest, as they say, is history.

8
GREATER HEIGHTS

Against all odds, I finally obtained my Geology degree in 1974. It was a moment of immense fulfillment—a triumph over years of relentless striving, struggles, and sacrifices. Every hardship I had endured, every deprivation I had faced, had been for this one goal, and at last, it had come to fruition.

My heart swelled with gratitude to God, and a profound sense of assurance filled me. With my degree in hand, I felt secure about my future, eager to launch my long-cherished career in the oil industry. More than that, I was emboldened with a newfound confidence—I had conquered this challenge, and I knew I could overcome even greater ones.

Still riding the wave of euphoria and self-assurance that came with earning my bachelor's degree, I applied for and was admitted into the graduate program at Wright State University in Dayton, Ohio, in the fall of 1975. I was accepted into the Master of Science (MSc) program in Geology and Geophysics. As an added blessing, I was offered a part-time faculty position as a Graduate Teaching Assistant in the Geology department.

However, the modest earnings from that position barely covered my tuition and living expenses. To make ends meet, I had to take on an additional part-time job at a computer center, working tirelessly to stay afloat financially.

Pursuing my master's degree proved to be another demanding endeavor, filled with rigorous coursework and the demanding research required for my thesis. Balancing full-time work with a graduate program was no small feat, especially with extremely limited financial resources. The obstacles were numerous—academic pressures, financial struggles, and material shortages—each one threatening to derail my progress. Yet, with rock-solid determination and faith, I pressed on.

In the end, by the grace of God, I successfully completed my master's degree.

CONJUGAL BLISS

About the same time that I obtained my master's degree, something more significant happened—I married the love of my life, Olawunmi. I had previously mentioned how God orchestrated our meeting during a summer vacation both of our families spent in Sapele in 1960. At the time, Wunmi was a student at Yejide Girls' Grammar School in Ibadan, having completed her primary education at Anglican Primary School, Ibadan.

From the moment we met, a strong connection was forged between us. We maintained consistent communication, seizing every opportunity to exchange letters. Even after I relocated to the United States for my undergraduate studies, our bond remained unshaken. Wunmi went on to attend Ibadan Grammar School for her Higher School Certificate (HSC) until 1966 before enrolling at Adeyemi College of Education in Ondo State.

Following her graduation, she briefly taught at Yejide Girls' Grammar School, Ibadan. However, in what

I can only describe as divine providence, she, too, was sent to the United States for her undergraduate studies. She attended Western Michigan University (WMU) in Kalamazoo, Michigan, where she pursued a Bachelor of Arts (BA) in French and English. This happened around the same time I was also working toward my undergraduate degree.

As someone who had been very close to Wunmi for years and who was more experienced with American life, I naturally took on a big-brother role for her. This dynamic strengthened our relationship even further. In another stroke of fate, she gained admission into Wright State University in the fall of 1975—the same university where I was pursuing my master's degree. She enrolled in a Master of Arts program in Education Curriculum and Instruction. Just like me, she was offered a part-time position as a Graduate Teaching Assistant in her department and supplemented her income with another part-time job in the university library.

Our time together during graduate school further affirmed everything I had always known about Wunmi. She was loving, generous, industrious, and unyielding in her pursuit of excellence. She worked tirelessly, often putting in late hours, yet never failed to extend kindness and care to those around her. She was a natural go-getter, deeply protective of the people she loved, and a woman of exceptional integrity. The more time I spent with her, the more captivated I became by her vibrant personality and extraordinary character. It became abundantly clear that I wanted to spend the rest of my life with her.

With certainty in my heart, I proposed to Wunmi, and she joyfully accepted. We subsequently informed our families back in Nigeria, and given that our families had been longtime friends, securing their blessings was relatively smooth. My family, the Idowu family in Ogbomoso, soon followed up with the traditional "idana" ceremony, during which the bride price and other customary requirements were fulfilled to the Odumosu family.

With all cultural and familial obligations met, and with the blessings of both families, Wunmi and I were soon married at the Harris County Courthouse in Houston, Texas. That day marked the beginning of a lifelong partnership built on love, mutual respect, and lifelong partnership.

SHOWERS OF BLESSING

Now, nearly fifty years later, I look back with immense gratitude to God for what remains one of the best decisions of my life. Wunmi has been my greatest confidant, motivator, and inspiration. She complements, completes, and consolidates my life in ways I never could have imagined. Through every high and low, every challenge and triumph, she has stood steadfastly by my side. To have walked this path with her has been one of the greatest joys of my existence.

Even more heartwarming is that God's abundant blessings have followed us every step of the way. Our marriage has not only endured but has flourished, growing richer with time. Among the greatest of these blessings are our six children and thirteen grandchildren, each a beautiful testimony to God's goodness. Their lives have brought us immeasurable joy, filling our home with warmth, love, and the unbreakable bonds of family.

Our grandchildren, in particular, have been a special source of delight. They are healthy, brilliant, and full of promise, bringing us unspeakable joy. Watching them grow and thrive has been one of the greatest rewards of our later years. Wunmi and I cherish every moment spent with them, relishing their laughter, their curiosity, and the love they so effortlessly pour into our lives. Whether gathered together in our home, sharing stories, or embarking on memorable family adventures, our time with them is always precious. Some of our most treasured experiences have been the ocean cruises we've taken together to the Mediterranean and Caribbean seas, as well as visits to breathtaking island resorts—often in celebration of their parents' birthdays. These moments have strengthened the bonds that hold us together and created a treasure trove of memories that will last a lifetime.

Among these remarkable grandchildren, our eldest granddaughter, an 18-year-old, has already begun carving out an extraordinary path. She gained admission to Baylor University in Waco, Texas, and in her very first semester in the fall of 2024, she achieved straight A's in all eight of her courses, excelling in her pre-medical studies. She is a gifted young woman and a role model to her younger siblings and cousins, who are equally brilliant in their own unique ways. Even our youngest grandchild, a lively and inquisitive seven-year-old, radiates intelligence and energy, reminding us that the future of our family is indeed bright.

What fills our hearts with the greatest joy, however, is not just their academic excellence but their strong faith and godly character. Each of them demonstrates a spirit of love, wisdom, and sound judgment, and we are eternally grateful to God for the privilege of watching them grow into the people He has destined them to be. We are deeply proud of every one of them and continue to lift them up in prayers, knowing that the Lord who has brought us this far will continue to guide and bless them.

Hallelujah! To God alone be all the glory.

PARTNERS IN EXCELLENCE

I recall that while Wunmi and I were still basking in the joy of our wedded life and journey into parenthood, we received yet another piece of thrilling news—we had both been accepted into doctoral programs at the University of Houston in Texas. It was an incredible opportunity, one that signified both personal and professional advancement.

I was admitted into a Ph.D. program in Geology, while my wife secured admission for a doctoral degree in Education. The moment was filled with joy, gratitude, and renewed determination. Yet, alongside the prestige and promise of higher education came daunting challenges, challenges that would test not only our resilience but also the strength of our marriage.

Pursuing a doctoral degree is no small feat, but pursuing one while raising children and working full-time is an entirely different level of challenge. Our days quickly became a nonstop cycle of responsibilities—attending classes, conducting research, completing assignments, meeting work obligations, and caring for our children. The pressure was intense, and at times, exhaustion weighed heavily on us.

There were moments when the strain tested our patience and resolve, but we were committed—not just to our individual successes but to our collective success as a family. We knew that we had to stay strong, support each other, and push forward together.

Despite our best efforts, however, it soon became clear that we couldn't handle everything on our own. The demands of our doctoral coursework, full-time jobs, and parenting were stretching us beyond our limits. After much deliberation, we made the difficult but necessary decision to hire a professional babysitter to handle the childcare aspect while we were away.

While this arrangement gave us the flexibility we needed, it came with a significant financial burden. Our income was already stretched thin between tuition, living expenses, and school-related costs, and now we had the added responsibility of paying for childcare. Still, we knew it was worth it.

Our daily routine became incredibly demanding. Weekdays were relentless. The only time we had to catch our breath was on weekends, and even then, we often spent that time preparing for the week ahead—studying, researching, and planning. The pace was unforgiving, but we knew that our sacrifices were temporary, while the rewards would last a lifetime.

As partners in progress, we remained committed to our shared vision. We encouraged each other, leaned on each other's strength, and endured the hardships with a firm belief in our future success. Despite the relentless demands, we pressed on with perseverance and faith. Between 1977 and 1978, we successfully completed our coursework for our doctoral programs—a significant milestone that propelled us toward the next phase: our research and dissertation work.

However, just as we were preparing to identify research topics, secure funding, and organize logistics for the next stage of our Ph.D. journey, some developments occurred back in Nigeria—developments so significant that they would alter the course of our plans and reshape our lives.

PER ARDUA AD ASTRA

9
HEEDING NIGERIA'S CALL TO SERVICE

Between 1975 and 1977, while I was deeply immersed in academic pursuits, adjusting to marriage, and embracing the responsibilities of fatherhood, momentous changes were unfolding back home in Nigeria, particularly in the oil industry. The country was at the peak of an oil boom, its economy surging with newfound wealth, and the government was determined to seize control of its own destiny.

At the heart of this government agenda were two major legislations: The Nigerian Enterprises Promotion

Decree (NEPD), also known as the indigenization policy; and Decree 33 of 1977.

The NEPD, which had been in motion since 1972, gained new momentum in 1977 with an aggressive push to transfer ownership and control of key industries into Nigerian hands. Through the amended NEPD, the indigenization policy expanded its reach, tightening restrictions on foreign dominance and reserving entire sectors for Nigerian citizens.

The oil industry, Nigeria's golden goose, became the center of this movement. Foreign oil giants were now required to relinquish substantial ownership stakes to Nigerians, ensuring that the country's vast petroleum resources would no longer be exploited without local participation.

To cement this shift, the government took an even bolder step by making Decree 33 of 1977. This legislation dismantled the Nigerian National Oil Corporation (NNOC) and merged it with the Federal Ministry of Petroleum Resources to form a single, more powerful entity: the Nigerian National Petroleum Corporation (NNPC). The new structure was designed to consolidate state control over oil exploration, production, and marketing, making it clear that Nigeria was no longer just an oil-producing nation but one that intended to own, manage, and profit from its resources.

However, while the vision was ambitious, it became obvious that Nigeria lacked enough qualified professionals to run the newly indigenized oil sector. The government quickly realized that if Nigerians were to take control, they needed to bring back their best minds from abroad. And so, a recruitment drive was launched, targeting Nigerian petroleum experts in the United States, Europe, and beyond. Government officials traveled to major oil capitals, including Houston, Texas, offering attractive contracts to entice skilled expatriates back home.

LUCRATIVE OFFERS

Faraway in Houston, my wife and I observed these developments with growing interest. The idea of returning home to serve, contribute, and build careers in a rapidly expanding industry felt both timely and compelling. While life in the U.S. had given us unparalleled education and exposure, it had also been a relentless grind—long hours, endless academic demands, and little time to truly settle into family life. The promise of something greater back home began to take hold of our hearts.

I submitted applications to several oil companies in Nigeria, and soon received three lucrative offers—one from Mobil Producing Nigeria (MPN), another from Gulf Oil Company, and a third from NNPC itself. The decision was not an easy one, but after weighing my options, I chose Mobil. Their offer was simply irresistible—a highly competitive salary, attractive benefits, and most importantly, full relocation support. Mobil would cover the cost of moving my entire family, including all our belongings in Houston, back to Nigeria. Beyond the financial appeal, I saw an opportunity to gain first-class industry experience in one of the world's most respected oil companies.

As God would have it, my wife also received an offer from the Federal Ministry of Education in Lagos to serve as an Education Officer. It was a moment of affirmation—everything we had worked for, every sacrifice we had made, was now leading us home.

Although accepting these opportunities meant putting our doctoral studies on hold, we knew it was the right decision. Our years in the U.S. had been about preparation, about laying the groundwork for something bigger. Now, that moment had arrived. The sacrifices we had made—the long nights, the financial struggles, the relentless pursuit of academic and professional excellence—were finally paying off. We were no longer just students chasing degrees; we were professionals stepping into high-impact roles that would allow us to serve our country and secure our family's future.

With a mixture of excitement and nostalgia, we packed our bags, said our goodbyes, and boarded our flight home. The land that had once sent us away for knowledge and experience was now welcoming us back—not as students, but as professionals, as contributors, as dreamers ready to take our place in the unfolding story of Nigeria's growth.

WINDS OF CHANGE

On my return to Nigeria with my family in 1978, I immediately realized that the Nigeria of that time stood in stark contrast to the one I left behind. As at 1970, the country was just emerging from the shadows of the devastating civil war, with the political landscape dominated by military rule, under General Yakubu Gowon. The nation was striving for unity and reconstruction, with a focus on healing the wounds inflicted by internal conflict. Economically, the country was primarily agrarian, with agriculture serving as the backbone of the economy. The discovery of oil had begun to hint at future prosperity, but its full impact was yet to be realized.

Between that time and 1978, however, the journey from post-war recovery to an oil-rich state had been swift and complex, marked by political upheavals, economic shifts, and profound social transformations. The once-prominent agricultural fields had been overshadowed by the rapid expansion of the oil industry, which had become the linchpin of the nation's economy. This oil boom had ushered in an era of unprecedented revenue, leading to ambitious infrastructure projects and urban development. Cities expanded, and new edifices dotted the skylines.

Politically, the landscape had been turbulent. The promise of a return to civilian rule had been deferred in 1974, leading to growing discontent. This unrest had culminated in the 1975 coup that ousted General Gowon, bringing General Murtala Mohammed to power. Mohammed's dynamic leadership was short-lived, as he was assassinated in 1976, leading to General Olusegun Obasanjo's ascent. Obasanjo steered the nation towards democracy, lifting the ban on political parties and overseeing the drafting of a new constitution in 1978, setting the stage for civilian governance.

Socially, the influx of oil wealth had a dual impact. While it spurred development and a sense of national pride, it also bred corruption and economic dependency. The rapid urbanization led to environmental challenges, particularly in the Niger Delta, where oil extraction had begun to take a toll on local ecosystems. The societal fabric was being rewoven, with traditional agrarian lifestyles giving way to urban sensibilities, and the allure of oil wealth influencing cultural norms and aspirations.

EXPLOITS IN NIGERIA'S OIL SECTOR

Stepping into the oil industry at that time felt like joining a battlefield where every player was racing to stake their claim. The Niger Delta was a hive of activity, with major multinational oil corporations aggressively prospecting and expanding production.

Mobil Producing Nigeria (MPN), Shell, Agip, ELF, Ashland, Pan Ocean, and a host of other companies had turned the region into a global oil hotspot.

At Mobil, I took up the role of Exploration/Production Geologist, assigned to Oil Mining Lease (OML) 67–70. The work was intense, demanding precision, innovation, and collaboration. I was part of a high-performing technical team, working alongside geophysicists, petroleum engineers, and financial analysts. Together, we conducted in-depth geological surveys, designed drilling strategies, and optimized oil field development to maximize production. The pressure was immense, but so was the satisfaction of knowing that we were shaping the future of Nigeria's most valuable industry.

After three years of rigorous work at Mobil, I reached a turning point. By then, I had gained a solid grasp of the technical and operational aspects of oil exploration and production. But deep within me, a stronger calling was emerging—to be part of something bigger, to help steer Nigeria's oil industry toward true national ownership and expertise. The indigenization policy had created opportunities for Nigerians to take the reins, and I felt it was time to step into that space. With this conviction, I made a bold move—I left Mobil to join the Nigerian National Petroleum Corporation (NNPC).

Working at NNPC was a uniquely fulfilling experience. Unlike Mobil, where my focus was on a single company's operations, NNPC placed me at the heart of Nigeria's joint venture (JV) partnerships with all the major multinational oil companies. I found myself navigating the complex web of agreements, negotiations, and financial structures that dictated how Nigeria's vast petroleum resources were managed. From Shell to Mobil (later ExxonMobil), ELF to Agip, I gained first-hand exposure to the diverse operational cultures and technological strategies of the world's biggest oil players. This experience expanded my expertise far beyond geology—it gave me insight into the global oil economy, corporate governance, and the high-stakes politics of resource management.

By the early 1980s, NNPC underwent a major restructuring, leading to the creation of National Petroleum Investment Management Services (NAPIMS)—a specialized division tasked with maximizing Nigeria's financial and operational interests in the oil industry. As a member of this elite unit, my role expanded further, overseeing joint venture operations, production sharing contracts (PSCs), and service contracts (SCs). We were not just managing resources; we were redefining how Nigeria engaged with multinational corporations, ensuring that the nation benefited fully from its oil wealth.

Every day at NNPC was a lesson in power, strategy, and economic diplomacy. I had the privilege of traveling extensively—from oil fields deep in the Niger Delta to corporate headquarters in Europe and the United States. The exposure was invaluable, reinforcing my belief that Nigeria's future lay in building a cadre of skilled professionals who could compete with the best in the global oil industry.

AN AVALANCHE OF REWARDS

This era of the Nigerian oil boom was not just professionally fulfilling for me but it was also a time of abundant blessings and divine favor in my family. As I ascended the ranks in my career, my personal life flourished beyond my wildest dreams.

But these joys brought greater responsibilities. As I mentioned above, my job required extensive travel—long weeks in remote oil fields, high-stakes meetings in Lagos, and international assignments in Europe and America. The demands of the job often kept me away from home, leaving my wife to shoulder the immense task of managing our growing family. She was the quiet force behind everything. Balancing her own career in education with the full-time responsibility of raising our ~~children, she embraced~~ the challenge with grace and resilience.

Looking back, I marvel at how much we endured and achieved. My dream of working in the oil industry had not only come true but had exceeded my wildest expectations. I was no longer just a student of geology—I was a key player in shaping Nigeria's oil future!

10
FURTHER EXPLOITS AT NNPC

As I reflect again on the entirety of my professional life, I can say without doubt that the journey was marked by courageous pursuits, extraordinary achievements, and defining moments—most of which were made possible only by the boundless grace of God Almighty. Time and again, God empowered me to rise beyond limitations, seize opportunities, and surpass expectations, even in moments when I wasn't fully aware of His guiding hand or certain of the path ahead.

Naturally, with NNPC being the place where I served the longest, most of these professional accomplishments happened during the time I worked there. Throughout those years, I was privileged to be involved in some of the most strategic technical and economic operations in Nigeria's oil industry

In addition to the instances that I already narrated in the previous chapter, I recall that during the joint venture participation period, spanning 1982 to 1996, I served as a geologist and geophysicist, working in a dynamic, multidisciplinary team alongside petroleum engineers, economists, and accountants. Our primary responsibility was to analyze and assess the exploration, development, and production economics of oil fields in the Niger Delta Basin. This required a delicate balance between scientific precision and economic feasibility, ensuring that Nigeria's stake in the oil industry was both profitable and sustainable.

Moreover, the nature of our work meant that our expertise was needed both domestically and internationally. Our teams frequently alternated between oil field operations in Nigeria and the home bases of multinational corporations abroad, where we engaged in high-level technical and economic discussions.

For instance, I was a key member of the professional teams that assessed Agip Oil's Joint Venture operations in Lagos and Milan, Italy. Later, I was involved in technical and economic evaluations for ELF Oil in Paris and Southern France and also participated in Shell Oil and Gas Company's operations in The Hague, Netherlands. These interactions provided valuable knowledge exchange between Nigerian professionals and foreign experts, equipping us with insights and cutting-edge technologies that would later play a critical role in the Federal Government's mission to indigenize Nigeria's oil industry.

Through these experiences, I gained a deep understanding of global oil and gas exploration strategies. I had the opportunity to work with some of the most advanced technologies of that time, observing how different multinational companies approached oil production and economic feasibility. Each engagement broadened my perspective, refining my technical expertise and reinforcing my belief that Nigeria had the capacity to become a leader in petroleum exploration—if only we could harness our resources effectively.

SHARING KNOWLEDGE AND TRAINING FUTURE EXPERTS

One of my greatest passions throughout my career was knowledge sharing. I strongly believed that whatever I learned should not stay with me alone—it had to be documented, shared, and passed on to others.

Each time I traveled abroad for technical operations, I saw it as an opportunity to study, reflect, and write. I dedicated time to documenting my observations and insights, turning them into technical papers and research reports. Over the years, I authored and published more than a dozen technical papers on oil field exploration, development, production, and economics in the Niger Delta Basin. Many of these were presented at conferences both within Nigeria and internationally, contributing to the growing body of knowledge in the petroleum sector.

In addition to writing, I was deeply involved in training and mentorship. I conducted workshops and seminars for colleagues within NNPC, ensuring that younger professionals were equipped with the latest industry knowledge. My passion for bridging academia and industry also led me to serve as an Adjunct Professor at Obafemi Awolowo University (OAU) and the

University of Jos (UNIJOS), where I helped integrate real-world oil and gas operations into their academic curriculum.

One of the most rewarding aspects of this role was seeing students who learned from my teachings secure positions in top oil companies, using the knowledge they had gained to advance Nigeria's petroleum sector. It was fulfilling to contribute not just to the present state of the industry but also to its future.

PIONEERING MARGINAL OIL FIELD DEVELOPMENT IN NIGERIA

Perhaps one of my most significant contributions to Nigeria's oil industry was my involvement in the establishment of Marginal Oil Field operations— an initiative aimed at expanding opportunities for indigenous participation in petroleum exploration and production.

As a member of the NAPIMS committee, I worked alongside a team of experts to propose and develop the framework for marginal oil field licensing. We recognized that while multinational corporations dominated Nigeria's oil sector, there were numerous smaller oil fields that remained untapped. Our vision was to withdraw these dormant fields from larger Oil Mining Leases (OMLs) and auction them to indigenous operators. This would allow local companies to develop the fields under more favorable fiscal terms, thereby boosting Nigeria's domestic oil production capacity and reducing dependency on foreign investors.

At the time, marginal oil field development was an emerging global trend, with many countries seeking to optimize production from smaller reservoirs. My research on this topic became a pivotal point in my career, leading to my first-ever international technical paper presentation.

In 1987, while serving as Chief Geologist/Geophysicist at NNPC in Lagos, I developed a technical abstract and proposal for a research paper titled "Marginal Oil Field Development and Economics in Nigeria." The paper explored the feasibility, fiscal policies, and economic implications of marginal oil production in Nigeria, offering insights into how government regulations could be structured to encourage investment in smaller fields.

The timing of the paper was perfect. The global petroleum industry was increasingly focused on enhanced oil recovery techniques and cost-effective production strategies, making my research highly relevant. The paper was accepted by the American Association of Petroleum Geologists (AAPG), and I was invited to present it at the North Pacific Conference in Honolulu, Hawaii, in 1987.

For me, this was a moment of both excitement and apprehension. While I had presented technical papers within Nigeria, this was my first opportunity to speak on a global stage before an audience that included CEOs, senior executives, and top petroleum experts from around the world.

NNPC and NAPIMS recognized the importance of this presentation and fully sponsored my trip to Hawaii. When the day finally came, I stood before the global oil industry's finest and delivered my presentation with confidence. The response was overwhelmingly positive. The research was well received, sparking discussions among policymakers and industry leaders on how emerging oil-producing nations could optimize their marginal oil field resources.

Following the conference, my paper was published in the Oil & Gas International Journal, making it a reference point for discussions on Nigeria's marginal oil field development initiatives.

RETIRED TO REFIRE

After nearly two decades of dedicated service to the Federal Government of Nigeria, my wife and I formally retired in 1996. It was a moment of deep reflection, gratitude, and celebration. Looking back, we could only marvel at the countless accomplishments, the grace that sustained us, and the numerous blessings that had shaped our journey. Retirement was not just about stepping away from active service; it was a time to acknowledge God's faithfulness and embrace the next phase of life. Hallelujah!

Naturally, we took some time to rest, reset, reflect, and seek God's direction on the next phase of our journey. We knew that retirement didn't mean giving up but pivoting to new possibilities. Soon, considering my years of experience and an in-depth understanding of the oil and gas industry, I began making plans to establish a consulting firm in Lagos. The goal was to use my wealth of knowledge to contribute to the industry in a new capacity.

However, just as we were mapping out our strategies, God intervened with a surprise—a door we never saw coming. Out of the blue, I received an offer from Western Atlas International, a leading oil services company, to work in Houston, Texas. Western Atlas had been formed in 1987 through the merger of Western Geophysical, owned by Litton Industries, and Dresser Atlas.

Interestingly, just as it was with the Mobil offer that brought us to Nigeria, this offer generously included a full relocation package, covering every aspect of moving our entire family back to the U.S. In essence, God was again placing an opportunity before us on a "platter of gold."

It was almost too incredible to believe. But there it was, an open door from God to step into another season of growth, impact, and adventure. With gratitude and enthusiasm, we began preparations for our move back to the United States.

PER ARDUA AD ASTRA

11

DIVINE AWAKENING

Following my acceptance of the Western Atlas offer, my family and I returned to the United States in 1996, stepping into what I believed was the next exciting phase of our lives. The move brought a sense of fulfillment for several reasons. First, the American system is structured to support senior citizens, allowing them to remain productive and contribute meaningfully to society. Second, it presented an opportunity for me to continue my professional career in Houston, Texas—the oil capital of the world. Most importantly, it gave my children access to one of the best education systems in the world, positioning them for a future full of opportunities.

Resuming work at Western Atlas itself felt like stepping into a perfect professional fit. I was assigned to an elite exploration and development team, where we handled data acquisition, processing, and interpretation for oil and gas reservoir projects. The work environment was dynamic and stimulating, and the company's exceptional employment package made it all the more rewarding.

Over time, I observed that the work culture at Western Atlas was highly competitive, with attractive incentives for employees who exceeded expectations. Performance-based rewards, career advancement opportunities, and financial benefits made it easy to get lost in the pursuit of success. I was determined to prove myself and contribute significantly to the company's growth, so I threw myself completely into my work, often working long hours, weekends, and late nights.

However, while I was focused on professional growth, God had a different plan for my life—one that would unfold in an unexpected way.

SPIRITUAL DRIFT: LOSING SIGHT OF GOD

Here is a little background to that drastic move of God in my life. Shortly after returning to the U.S., my family and I were invited to the inauguration of The Redeemed Christian Church of God (RCCG), Restoration Chapel Parish, in Houston, Texas. The dedication was conducted by Pastor Enoch Adeboye, the General Overseer of RCCG, from its Lagos headquarters. Under the leadership of Pastor Dave Okunade and Pastor Kamal Sanusi (of blessed memory), we became active members, attending weekly services and participating in church programs.

However, as my workload at Western Atlas increased, my commitment to spiritual activities started to wane. As I mentioned above, the company placed a high premium on performance, and employees were encouraged to put in extra hours to secure promotions and financial rewards. I became engrossed in meeting company targets, often working weekends in pursuit of greater financial rewards and career progression.

Before long, I began skipping mid-week Bible study and fellowship meetings. Then, gradually, Sundays became workdays too. What started as an occasional absence from church became a habitual neglect of spiritual responsibilities. My devotion to God was replaced by devotion to career advancement. Outreach evangelism, welfare service, tithing, and thanksgiving offerings all took a back seat. I had unknowingly relegated my spiritual life to the margins, focusing solely on climbing the corporate ladder.

I told myself I was simply working hard to secure a better future for my family, but in reality, I had substituted my spiritual priorities for material pursuits.

THE WAKE-UP CALL

About two years into this phase of my life, God allowed circumstances to shake me awake. The life I had so carefully built around career and financial security began to crumble.

First, financial pressures mounted in ways I hadn't expected. Despite my good earnings, expenses increased disproportionately, creating unexpected financial strain. My health also took a hit, with frequent episodes of stress-induced illnesses.

I assumed the solution was to work even harder, believing that if I put in more hours, I could outwork the challenges. But around this time, Western Atlas introduced new performance demands due to the global economic downturn in the oil and gas industry. There were whispers of layoffs, and employees were expected to increase productivity or risk termination.

This intensified my anxiety, pushing me to work longer hours with little rest. But instead of improving my situation, it left me physically drained and emotionally exhausted.

Then came the breaking point.

One evening, after leaving the office late at night, I was involved in a ghastly auto accident. A fire truck struck my SUV at an intersection, causing my vehicle to flip over multiple times before coming to a total stop. The car was completely wrecked, but miraculously, I survived. Hallelujah!

RECUPERATION AND REGENERATION

Lying on my hospital bed, I was forced to confront the reality of my life. For the first time in years, I paused to reflect. I saw how I had drifted away from

God, prioritizing worldly achievements over my spiritual well-being. I had neglected the One who had consistently carried me through life's challenges.

In deep humility, I repented and cried out to God. I asked Him to fully take control of my life and give me a fresh start. I surrendered my whole being, vowing to serve Him fully and wholeheartedly.

The day I was discharged from the hospital marked a new beginning. I rededicated my life to God, immersing myself in prayer, Bible study, and church service. The more I sought God, the more I realized how empty my life had been without Him.

One scripture became my personal anthem during this period:

"For what shall it profit a man, if he shall gain the whole world, and lose his own soul?" *(Mark 8:36, KJV)*

I had been chasing success, but in the process, I had almost lost my soul. From that moment on, I saw my life through a different lens. Everything about my life was simply a tool for God's greater purpose. I became more involved in the church, dedicating time to evangelism, mentorship, and service. My spiritual hunger deepened, and my relationship with God flourished like never before. The Scripture became fulfilled in my life: "Therefore, if anyone is in Christ, he is a new creation; old things have passed away; behold, all things have become new." *(2 Corinthians 5:17, NKJV)*

I was no longer the same man who had walked through the doors of Western Atlas consumed by self-ambition. God had repositioned me for a greater purpose, and this time, I was ready to follow His lead.

NEW LIFE, NEW FOCUS

Realizing that I couldn't sustain my renewed relationship with God while hadling the demanding pressures of my job at Western Atlas, I made the bold decision in 1998 to resign and focus on strengthening my spiritual life and overall well-being. It was a leap of faith, but God, in His faithfulness, soon provided me with a part-time academic lectureship—a role that not only enriched my spiritual journey but also significantly improved my health.

Interestingly, teaching had always been my long-term aspiration. My plan had been to gain practical industry experience in the oil and gas sector before transitioning into academia, where I could mentor and inspire young professionals. I had drawn inspiration from my graduate school professors at Wright State University in Dayton, Ohio, and the University of Houston, many of whom worked in the oil industry before retiring into teaching. Their ability to bridge industry practice with academic training fascinated me, and I aspired to follow a similar path.

It was this same passion for academia that had driven me to serve as an Adjunct Professor at Obafemi Awolowo University, Ile-Ife, and the University of Jos between 1983 and 1996, during my time in Nigeria. So, stepping into a teaching role after leaving Western Atlas felt like a natural progression, one that aligned with my divine calling and professional passion.

I started teaching Geology on a part-time basis at Houston Community College (HCC) while also working as a substitute teacher at Alief Independent School District (AISD). Around the same time, I finally launched the consulting firm I had originally planned to establish when I first retired in Nigeria in 1996. The company, Jamemil Services International, was set up to train Nigerian professionals in the oil industry. It was a fulfilment of the vision I had shared with my colleagues at NNPC-NAPIMS before retiring from public service.

I partnered with a business associate in Nigeria, who recruited professionals from oil companies and other organizations for specialized training programs. These professionals—geologists, geophysicists, petroleum engineers, accountants, economists, financial administrators, and medical doctors—were flown to Houston for targeted workshops in their respective fields. Jamemil Services International in Houston served as the training coordinator, ensuring the programs met international industry standards.

For a few years, our operations thrived, providing cutting-edge training and bridging knowledge gaps between Nigerian professionals and global industry practices. However, by the year 2000, the general downturn in the oil industry had taken a serious toll on our business and I decided to fully commit to my teaching career.

PIONEERING ONLINE GEOLOGY EDUCATION

At Houston Community College (HCC), I became deeply involved in developing innovative ways to enhance the learning experience for students. In 2003, I designed and launched the first-ever online course in Physical Geology (GEOL 1403)—a pioneering effort that significantly expanded access to geology education.

In 2005, I was offered a full-time position as a Geology professor at the University of Houston-Downtown (UHD). There, I continued my passion for academic innovation, launching online courses in Meteorology, Oceanography, and Climate Studies in 2008. These courses have since become fundamental subjects within the Natural Sciences curriculum at both HCC and UHD.

To this day, I remain an Adjunct Geology Professor at HCC and a Lecturer in the Natural Science Department at UHD, where I continue to train, mentor, and inspire students in their academic and professional pursuits.

A PLATFORM FOR MENTORSHIP AND MINISTRY

One of the greatest blessings of my academic career has been the direct engagement with students from diverse backgrounds. Since 2000, I have had the privilege of mentoring students—not just academically, but also spiritually and personally.

Many of my students have approached me with questions about life, faith, and career. I have found countless opportunities to encourage, counsel, and guide them, helping them navigate spiritual, academic, and personal challenges. Some have come to me thirsting for deeper meaning, and I have been able to point them to God, sharing my testimony of how faith has shaped my journey.

Beyond the classroom, I also became more active in evangelism and community outreach. From the moment I walked away from the oil industry to prioritize my faith, my peace of mind improved, my health stabilized, and my sense of purpose deepened.

"But seek first the kingdom of God and His

righteousness, and all these things shall be added to you." *(Matthew 6:33, NKJV)*

Indeed, my decision to prioritize God over professional ambition opened greater doors than I could have ever imagined. I had thought I was leaving behind a thriving career, but in reality, I was stepping into a higher calling—one that would allow me to impact lives for eternity.

12
DEEPER FELLOWSHIP AND SPIRITUAL SERVICE

With my priorities now shifted away from secular success, my heart became fully immersed in the work of the Kingdom. I found greater purpose, fulfillment, and joy in serving God, and every aspect of my life began to align with this new focus. My family and I embraced this journey wholeheartedly, dedicating ourselves to ministry and service in ways that strengthened our faith and deepened our commitment to Christ.

While we were still members of RCCG Restoration Parish, I actively taught Sunday School, sharing biblical insights with other believers. My wife, equally devoted, served in the Children's Department, nurturing the young ones in the ways of the Lord. Our children also found their places in the ministry, serving as ushers and workers, making us a family wholly committed to God's work.

A NEW HOME IN RCCG

In 2001, we transitioned to RCCG Living Word Chapel (LWC), led by Senior Pastor Dave Arogbonlo. The decision was mainly due to its nearness to our home but it also turned out to be a divine positioning for deeper spiritual growth and leadership. Since joining LWC, I have served as the Sunday School Coordinator, while my wife became an active member of the Women's Fellowship Group, encouraging and mentoring other women in their faith journeys.

As the church continued to grow, I was privileged to be part of a pioneering initiative to strengthen fellowship among the elders across RCCG parishes in Houston. Following the guidance of the church's leadership, Elder Michael Adeeko and I were used by God to establish the RCCG Elders Group of Houston, a network that sought to foster unity and collective prayer among elders across all sister churches.

At the time, RCCG had over 50 parishes in Houston, and our goal was to bring the elders together in one accord, strengthening their spiritual lives and encouraging a deeper sense of community. Through prayers, praise, and testimonies, we saw God work mightily, answering prayers and bringing healing and restoration to many souls. To this day, we continue to glorify God for the unity and strength He has brought to this group.

DEEPER SCRIPTURAL KNOWLEDGE

By 2007, I was filled an increasing desire to consolidate my spiritual growth with a more structured study of the Bible. Around this time, my son, Pastor Tunde, discovered the Whole Life Success Ministry Institute (WLSMI) in Houston, Texas, a Bible college founded by Bishop Hazel Hughes. Impressed by the depth of its curriculum and the quality of teaching, he enrolled with the goal of deepening his knowledge of scripture in preparation for pastoral ministry.

Shortly after beginning his studies, he shared his experience with me, urging me to join. As I listened to my son's excitement and reflected on my own desire to grow in God's Word, I felt compelled to enroll on a part-time basis.

What began as a simple step toward learning soon became one of the best decisions of my life. Under Bishop Hughes and a team of anointed instructors, I found myself immersed in rigorous study of the Bible, examining the Old and New Testaments with fresh eyes. Each lesson revealed deeper insights into scripture, challenging me to apply biblical principles in ways I had never considered before.

Throughout the program, we explored various translations of the Bible, studying how each version captured the essence of the original texts. Weekly assessments kept us engaged, while guest ministers and external Christian seminars exposed us to different perspectives on ministry and faith. In addition to learning foundational and advanced biblical concepts, we studied the lives and teachings of renowned Christian leaders, analyzing their preaching styles and spiritual impact.

The program also required practical participation—attending prayer encounters, freedom workshops, and structured Bible-reading plans—which helped reinforce everything we learned. One of the most challenging but rewarding aspects was writing a biblical thesis, a task that pushed me to articulate my faith and personal experiences in light of scripture.

Beyond the structured coursework, Bishop Hughes brought in guest ministers and organized various Christian seminars, ensuring that we were exposed to diverse perspectives on faith and ministry.

On January 10, 2009, Pastor Tunde and I graduated together. While he went on to become the Senior Pastor of Rejuvenation Church in Houston, Texas, I continue serving at RCCG Living Word Chapel, where I remain the Sunday School Coordinator and Minister in charge of the Elders' Fellowship. The experience at WLSMI proved to be not just a theological training but a divine encounter that deepened my faith and prepared me for greater service in God's vineyard.

LIFE-CHANGING PILGRIMAGE TO THE HOLY LAND

One of the most memorable experiences of my spiritual journey came in 2015, when my wife and I embarked on a pilgrimage to the Holy Land. For years, we had longed to visit the sacred sites where biblical history unfolded, to walk in the very places where Jesus lived, preached, and performed miracles. When the opportunity finally arose, we knew it was God's appointed time.

The moment we set foot in Jerusalem, we were overwhelmed by a deep sense of reverence. We visited Nazareth, the birthplace of Jesus, and stood on Mount Olivet, where He often prayed. At Gethsemane, we reflected on the night of His agonizing prayer before His betrayal. Our journey took us to Mount Carmel, the site of Elijah's dramatic encounter with the prophets of Baal, and to Cana of Galilee, where Jesus performed His first miracle at a wedding feast.

We stood by the Dead Sea, marveled at the Sea of Galilee, and visited the ancient Jerusalem Church and Sepulcher. Walking along the Via Dolorosa, the path Jesus took to His crucifixion, was a deeply moving experience, and standing on Golgotha (Calvary) where He was crucified filled us with an indescribable solemnity.

The most unforgettable moment of our pilgrimage was our baptism in the Jordan River, where Jesus Himself was baptized. As we emerged from the water, I felt a renewed sense of purpose and a fresh outpouring of God's presence. Holding our baptismal certificates, we rejoiced, knowing that this journey had not only been a historical experience but also a spiritual encounter that deepened our walk with Christ.

Returning from the Holy Land, I found myself reading the Bible with greater clarity. The places I had once only imagined through scripture were now real to me, making my study of the Word even more meaningful.

PER ARDUA AD ASTRA

13

FROM SCIENCE TO SCRIPTURE: JOURNEY INTO KINGDOM WRITING

As I previously mentioned, by the time I retired from an active and exciting career in the petroleum industry in 1998, I had already made significant contributions to my field, having published over a dozen technical papers on petroleum exploration, development, and production economics. These publications, built upon cutting-edge research and industry advancements, had earned me recognition in professional circles. However, despite my proficiency in technical writing, I struggled with an unfulfilled desire—the urge to write a scriptural book.

For years, the thought lingered in my heart, but I lacked the conviction to begin. It was not that I doubted my ability to write; rather, I wrestled with an overwhelming sense that spiritual writing required a level of divine insight and maturity that I was yet to attain. Whenever I considered putting pen to paper, I questioned whether I had enough spiritual depth to produce something meaningful. Was I equipped to write a book that would truly edify believers? Would my words carry the weight of revelation, or would they merely echo intellectual knowledge without the power of the Holy Spirit?

PROPHETIC IGNITION

This internal struggle continued until a pivotal moment on June 14, 2017. During our regular Bible Study session at RCCG Living Word Chapel (LWC) in Houston, Texas, Pastor Dave Arogbonlo made a prophetic declaration that would change everything.

During the question-and-answer segment of the study, he suddenly paused, walked directly toward me, and, looking me in the eye, said, *"God said you are to write a book. What are you waiting for? And I don't mean your professional science book!"*

The words pierced through me like a sword. At that moment, I knew this was not just an encouragement from a pastor; it was a direct message from God. The prophecy spoke to the very hesitation I had battled for years, exposing my excuses and reaffirming my calling.

Immediately, my mind was drawn to Habakkuk 2:2-3, which states:

"Then the Lord answered and said: 'Write the vision and make it plain on tablets, that he may run who reads it. For the vision is yet for an appointed time, but at the end it will speak, and it will not lie. Though it tarries, wait for it; because it will surely come, it will not tarry.'"

RUNNING WITH THE CHARGE

I received the message with all my heart, personalized it, and ran with it. The call was clear—I was to write, not just as an intellectual exercise, but as an act of obedience to God.

As I reflected further, I realized that the main reason I had been unable to write scriptural books was because I had been trying to approach scriptural writing the same way I had approached technical writing. But writing for God is an entirely different "ball game." Unlike my professional papers, which relied on research, logic, and scientific principles, a scriptural book has to be Spirit-filled, rooted in divine revelation, and centered on Jesus Christ.

Once I grasped this truth, my perspective shifted. I prayed sincerely for God's help, and He liberated me from the fears that had held me back. I no longer saw writing a scriptural book as a daunting intellectual task but as a spiritual assignment—one that would be fueled by divine inspiration rather than human effort.

With a newfound sense of courage and confidence, I began my first book. The process was deeply remarkable. As I wrote, the Holy Spirit guided my thoughts, providing insight and clarity that I knew did not originate from me alone. The words flowed with ease, and before long, my first book was completed.

To my amazement, after completing my first book, the inspiration to write more followed almost immediately. Within two years, I had written and published four books, each one addressing different dimensions of the Christian walk. This was beyond what I had imagined possible, and I knew it was nothing but the grace of God.

To the glory of God, my journey from hesitation to obedience has resulted in a powerful outpouring of wisdom, testimonies, and scriptural revelations that I am privileged to share with the world.

This understanding fuels my passion for writing. My goal is not just to document my experiences but to encourage others—to inspire them to hold on to their faith, to never give up, and to always trust in God's perfect timing.

I firmly believe that everyone has a God-given assignment, and when we surrender to His leading, He equips us beyond our limitations. The same God who took a former petroleum engineer and transformed him into a scriptural author can do the same and even more for anyone who yields to His call.

MY SCRIPTURAL BOOKS

Through divine inspiration, I have written and published the following four books, all available on Amazon.com and Kindle:

1. The Power of Confession (Unveiling the

Power of Spoken Words)

Have you ever considered that the words you speak shape your destiny? This book explores the profound impact of the words we speak. Many people underestimate the power of their tongue, not realizing that their confessions shape their reality. Scripture makes it clear that words have the power to build, destroy, create, or limit our lives. In this book, I reveal how spoken words influence our destiny and how believers can align their confessions with God's promises. I share personal experiences of how divine confessions changed impossible situations in my life and how anyone can activate miraculous breakthroughs through faith-filled words. This book is a guide to speaking life, attracting favor, and transforming your future through the power of the tongue.

2. Dominion Lifestyle (Living the Life of Heaven on Earth)

This book calls believers to fully embrace their Kingdom authority. Many Christians live far below their divine potential, struggling with fear, failure, and defeat, unaware that they have been given power to reign. This book reveals how to unlock the supernatural strength within, teaching believers how to live victoriously every day. It outlines the principles of kingdom living, showing how to break free from the limitations of the world's system and step into a realm of divine abundance, peace, and success. Through this book, I encourage every believer to see themselves the way God sees them—as conquerors, rulers, and overcomers.

3. Winning Virtues (Success Principles of Kingdom Champions)

This book delves into the qualities that distinguish fruitful believers from stagnant ones. What makes the difference between a life of impact and a life of mediocrity? What separates champions from those who merely exist? This book explores the virtues that lead to success in both the spiritual and physical realms. Many people assume that zeal alone is enough to thrive in God's kingdom, but true success requires knowledge, commitment, and discipline. I emphasize the importance of spiritual growth, consistency, and perseverance in fulfilling God's purpose. Using real-life testimonies, I show how applying these winning virtues can transform ordinary believers into extraordinary vessels for God's glory.

4. The Living Church (Church Takes a Whole New Dimension!)

The church is more than just a building—it is a living, breathing body, empowered by the Holy Spirit to impact the world. This book provides deep insights into God's original plan for His Church. Many believers attend church without fully understanding its purpose and power. This book sheds light on what the Church was truly meant to be—a movement of Spirit-filled believers impacting lives. I discuss the fundamental doctrines that the Church must be built upon, strategies for igniting revival, empowering church members, and keeping the fire of faith burning. This book challenges believers to shake off limiting beliefs and embrace the true power and calling of the Church.

OVERALL MESSAGE

Each of these books carries a unique message of faith, victory, and transformation. They are not just words on pages, but life-changing revelations meant to equip believers for a deeper walk with God. I encourage anyone who desires to grow spiritually, walk in victory, and discover their divine purpose to read them and apply the principles within.

I am deeply grateful for the privilege of sharing these messages with the world. My prayer is that each reader will be encouraged, empowered, and transformed, understanding that their words, faith, and obedience have the power to shape their destinies in Christ.

To God be all the glory!

CLOSING THOUGHTS

As I conclude this narrative of my life's journey so far, my heart overflows with gratitude for the faithfulness of God. Eighty years of life have given me countless testimonies of His grace, mercy, and miraculous victories. Every challenge I have overcome, every trial I have faced, and every lesson I have learned has only deepened my conviction that God is ever-present and ever-faithful.

If there is one truth that life has impressed upon me, it is that the road to greatness is never smooth. Challenges will arise, hardships will come, and adversity will test the very foundations of your faith and resolve. Yet, woven into these struggles are opportunities for growth, refinement, and the unfolding of God's divine plan.

I have come to understand that perseverance, passion, and an unwavering focus on life's ultimate purpose are non-negotiable keys to fulfilling destiny. The process may be long and arduous, but for those who trust in

God and refuse to surrender to despair, there is always light at the end of the tunnel.

Beyond my personal experiences, I find it necessary to remind every believer and the body of Christ that the Scriptures are true, every word breathed by God for our guidance. The book of Revelation, in particular, stands as a solemn reminder that Jesus Christ is coming soon. It is not enough to know this; we must live in readiness, aligning our lives with His commandments and walking in holiness. The call is urgent. Our faith is not meant to be a passive declaration but a daily commitment to righteousness, love, and unwavering trust in God's promises.

With the privilege of hindsight, I can boldly affirm that God is real, alive, and ever present in our lives. His love is boundless, His faithfulness unshakable, and His power unmatched. None of us can accomplish anything by our own strength, yet in Him, all things are possible. He has carried me through valleys, lifted me over mountains, and continually proven that He is the God of all seasons.

As I close this chapter, I do so with a heart full of thanksgiving. My life has been a testament to God's grace, and I hope that my story inspires others to trust Him more deeply, to persevere through their trials, and to walk boldly in faith. Whatever challenges you may face, never forget this: with God, the stars are never out of reach. Hallelujah!

Wife and I celebration of 2019 Christmas with Grandchildren in Houston, Texas

My Dad, Mum, Auntie, and Siblings in the early 1940s at Ado-Ekiti, Nigeria

My Dad, Mum, and Siblings Christmastime 1960 at Sapele Mid-West, Nigeria

Dedication & Signing of My Scriptural Books 2018 at Living Word Chapel, Houston, Texas

My Wife and I during 2018 Book Dedication & Signing at Living Word Chapel, Houston Texas

Three-Generation Family photo 2018 Book Dedication & Signing at living Word Chapel, Houston, Texas

Early 1940s with Siblings at Ado-Ekiti, Nigeria

Science Major Classmates 1965 at Olivet Baptist High School, Oyo

My Wife and I graduated 1977 at Wright State University, Dayton, Ohio Graduate School

1976 Graduate School days at Dayton, Ohio

Photo with Prof. Akande, Vice-Chancelor UNILORIN at 1994 AAPG International Conference, Nice, France

Worshiping at RCCG Restoration Chapel Inauguration 1997, Houston, Texas

Surprise Birthday Celebration for My Wife by Restoration Chapel, Houston, Texas

My Family's Sunday Service worship 1999 at Restoration Chapel, Houston, Texas

2009 Bible College Graduation with Son Tunde at Whole Life Success Ministry Institute (WSMI), Houston Texas

2015 Water Baptism with Wife at River Jordan, Israel, Holy Land

2015 Visit with Wife to Birthplace of Lord Jesus Christ, Nazareth, Holy Land

Join us to celebrate the birthday of

Professor Ayorinde Idowu

RCCG Living Word Chapel	2nd of May 2015
13833 Richmond Ave, Houston, TX, 77082	2pm

Reception follows at Ayva Center
9371 Richmond Ave, Houston, TX. 77063

2015 Prof. Ayorinde Idowu, University of Houston, Downtown (UHD) at 70th Birthday Anniversary

2004DaughterTemitope'sweddingatLivingWord Chapel, Houston, Texas

2009daughterDolapo'sweddingatLivingword Chapel, Houston, Texas.

2015PaperPresentationatGeophysicalConference in Seatle, Washington

2017atWife's70thBirthdaycelebration,Houston, Texas.

Daughter Dolapo's Wedding Reception 2009
Houston, Texas

Daughter'sTemitope'sWeddingReception2004at
Houston, Texas.

Grandchildren Toddler Days Christmas Season 1990s at Houston, Texas.

Family's Christmas season late 1980s in Lagos, Nigeria.

My 70th Birthday Celebration 2015 with Three-Generation Family at living Word Chapel, Houston, Texas.

Elder Idowu's 70th Birthday 2015 with Three-Generation family in Houston, Texas.

Prof. Ayorinde Idowu with wife 2015 at 70th Birthday Anniversary, Houston, Texas

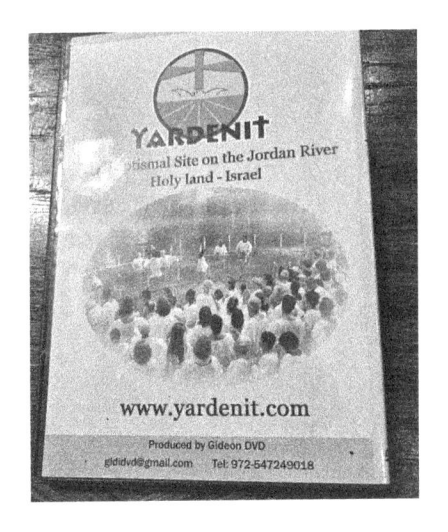

My Wife and I Water Baptism at YARDENIT Baptismal Site on Jordan River, Holy Land-Israel.

Idowu Siblings: Tunde, Tope, Fisayo, and Dolapo at 2025 Party reception in Houston, Texas

Ogbomosho Anglican Diocese Cathedral Old Church (from 1930s); and New Cathedral being renovated in 2024.

2024 Snapshot Christmas present

2023 Sea Cruise with Three-Generation Family on board Caribbean Cruise Ship, offshore Gulf Coast, U. S. A.